PRAISE FOR
THE KITCHEN IS CLOSED

"Sandra Butler once again demonstrates deft skill and daring observation in her deeply personal essays about being old. Reflecting on her life thus far, Sandra generously reveals her internal world as it relates to the state of her aging body, sexuality, friendships travel, and even her fashion choices. In Sandra's capable hands, these reflections make visible both the positive and painful experiences that many older women endure in silence, especially in a society characterized by ageism and misogyny.

"Sandra's greatest contribution to social and political life has been to break silences. She did this with her early writing on incest and in her cowriting with her dying partner describing the loss of one's great love.

"In this recent collection of essays, Sandy strips away any lingering avoidance some of us may have in confronting aging and offers us the gentle salve of her insights, humor, and wisdom."

—Dr. Lori Haskell, clinical psychologist

"Sandra Butler's *The Kitchen Is Closed: And Other Benefits of Being Old* takes on the subject of women and aging with piercing honesty and life-affirming gusto. This is not a somber 'what you should expect' or 'how you should feel' journey. Instead we experience life as she experiences it—with wisdom and humor that reflect both the challenges and the joys of one woman's passage into elderhood. This book is a must read for people of all ages. And, over and above its wisdom, it is a joy to read and enjoy the company of this beautiful narrative voice."

—Janet L. Holmgren, president emerita, Mills College

"*The Kitchen Is Closed* is a tenderhearted, funny compendium of stories, memories, and musings about aging, feminism, spirituality, culture, politics, and the body. Sandra Butler's memoir is unambiguously Jewish, salty, and occasionally wistful as she reflects with unrepentant honesty about her life as a mother, activist, friend, writer, lover of jazz, and citizen of the world. Her storytelling is imbued with warmth, well-earned sovereignty, and a sprinkling of humility."

—Karen Erlichman, spiritual director, LCSW, DMin

"As I read Butler's collection, I began a mental list of all the women I want to send this book to—as a road map, as a reminder to be just this tender, brave, witty, and self-accepting when we reach our eighties. Her writing illuminates how we all might inhabit our old age with curiosity, courage, and a well-developed sense of humor."

—Penny Rosenwasser, activist, educator, and author of *Hope into Practice: Jewish Women Choosing Justice Despite Our Fears*

"At last—a wise and witty romp through old age with nothing off-limits! Butler's deep dive is an invitation to recognize what it looks like to live an old life—on purpose."

—Rochelle Lefkowitz, founder and president, Pro-Media Communications; cofounder, Elder Action

The Kitchen Is Closed

SANDRA BUTLER

The Kitchen Is Closed

AND OTHER BENEFITS OF BEING OLD

BOTH/AND PRODUCTIONS

Copyright © 2022 by Sandra Butler

All rights reserved.

No part of this book may be reproduced, or stored in a retrieval system, or transmitted in any form or by any means, electronic, mechanical, photocopying, recording, or otherwise, without express written permission of the publisher.

Published by Both/And Productions, Phoenix, AZ
sandrabutler.net

Edited and designed by Girl Friday Productions
www.girlfridayproductions.com

Cover design: Anna Curtis
Project management: Kristin Duran
Editorial production: Abi Pollokoff
Image credits: cover © iStock Photo/Kemter

ISBN (paperback): 979-8-9857560-0-5
ISBN (e-book): 979-8-9857560-1-2

Library of Congress Control Number: 2022902989

To Marcia Freedman z"l

Who lived her old-womanness unapologetically with the exuberance, passion, outrage, and tenderness that characterized her life. Her memory will forever be a blessing.

And to my daughters, Janaea and Alison

You are my everything.

CONTENTS

INTRODUCTION

I'm not a woman who is older. Or elderly. Or mature. I'm neither plucky nor a burden, and not over any hills (except the very steep ones). I am a very specific old to be sure, white, once middle class, now a full economic level down from there, once tall and now several inches less than that. It appears that some things shrink over the years as others expand.

The questions I ask myself have shifted. What's it like to have a body that is starting to break down, a mind that is becoming more porous, finances that feel precarious? What is it I value? How do I define a good day? What's the changing nature of my friendships, many of which are decades long? What matters has shifted. So much that seemed crucial and fueled my middle-aged life—being successful, admired, chosen, productive—has fallen away, leaving in its wake a vast rush of relief.

Of course, there are real-life demands. The shoulds and the oughts are still alive and well in their persistence. I still have to dust my furniture. Water my plants. Wash my dishes. Try to touch my toes. Wash my hair. Floss my teeth. Pay my bills.

Unlike middle-aged Michelle Obama, I'm no longer becoming. I've become. My children are middle aged and continuing to grow into their fullness. I, on the other hand, have reached what appears to be the maximum level of my maturity, and while I'm more adult in public than I am in private, this has always been the case. I'm not nearly as kind as I intended to become, but at least greatly improved from the earnest young woman who valued certainty over ambiguity. I'm less evaluative about how and why people behave as they do, because I've learned over and over again how tremendously complicated it is to be a human being. I'm still vain, although I wish I weren't. Mostly about my hair. While my discipline is somewhat improved, my adventurousness remains on the timid side. Knowing what to expect, insofar as that is possible, still comforts me. But I keep reaching for my best self, and finally I am clear about who that self is. I bump against ageism in the ways people relate to me and to the reality of oldness, much as I once learned to more clearly identify and recognize racism and sexism. However, there are a lot of things that are funny about being old, but only if an old woman tells them.

There are intermittent moments when I'm happy to accept the social perks of oldness—special shopping hours, early boarding on planes, discounts at movies. But those well-earned advantages are all too often diminished by young people who, when they check out my groceries, welcome me on board, or sell me a movie ticket, refer to me as *dear, hon,* or *sweetie.* Then, using my full height, which is less full than it was ten years ago, but still on the formidable side, I look down at the offending youth and wait for them to recognize the appropriate shame at their presumptuous behavior. It works about a third of the time.

I keep myself in the best shape I can, am proud when I have accumulated enough "steps" at the end of the day, and sometimes walk up and down the halls of my apartment building for a few minutes to round the number up to the nearest thousand. My body is moving along toward the end, and I'm inside it, trying to be a friendly caretaker. Being careful is a requirement of oldness more than it was when I was merely young-old. I keep my phone with me all the time now—just in case.

I delight in the freedom that oldness confers, at least the freedom not to care about so many of the things that once seemed so important. I'm contentedly set in most of my hard-won ways. While I understand that being set can be interpreted as timid or rigidly unwilling to try something new—like watercolors, ballroom dancing, choral singing, line dancing, or gardening—that time came and instantly evaporated. I have become fond of my ways since it took so many decades to figure out what they were. They're what remains after years of painful, grudging, and fearful release of self-protective behaviors and choices, all of which involved psychotherapy, foolish relationships, and way too many gin and tonics. My ways make sense to me. And perhaps if Frank Sinatra hadn't gotten there first, I might have titled this book *My Ways*.

My eighteen-year-old self wouldn't recognize me. Eager to become an adult, I married a man with whom I expected to spend my life; raise our children; work at something that would hopefully provide me with satisfaction and purpose; and learn to garden, cook, and maybe eventually speak a second language fluently and even travel to where it is spoken. My 1956 imagination didn't extend past those generic dreams.

My children's father and I have been divorced for over sixty years. I never gardened and continue to be a pedestrian cook. My French consists of the rudiments, although I did get to spend time in France, using my limited phrases, smiling and pointing. The life I thought I was preparing for never arrived. Instead, another unfolded with unexpected openings, gifts, and catastrophes. Nothing I anticipated came to pass. But so much else did. So much I could never have imagined—rich, startling, melancholy, and triumphant.

These days, I inhabit a world where people have practices. Spiritual ones. Yogic ones. Psychological ones. I've been old for a while now, so it seems fitting that I design a personal practice of oldness. But I'm filled with wanting, and practices frown on desirousness of all kinds. I want to accompany my friends as they approach the end of their lives. I want to see how things turn out politically in these unimaginable times. I want to take walks by the water, even as those walks get increasingly slower, punctuated by longer periods of sitting and augmented by hiking poles. I want to read, have long talks with loved ones, keep fresh flowers on my coffee table. Practices are more focused on yielding to what is, with the emphasis on the here and now.

While I appear to be an unruly candidate to begin a practice, already chafing against the constraints of cultivating a sense of awe at each new moment (never ever going to happen), the evaporation of my memory does lend an often-bewildered openness. So, in the oft-repeated movement that Jews have been practicing for centuries, I lift my shoulders in a small shrug and remind myself that what I want has nothing to do with anything. It's going to be how I manage whatever comes. That central reality is embedded in teachings of spirituality and psychology, so I will now consider myself in the throes of a practice. Here I go.

LEARNING TO IMPROVISE

ONE

"Besame Mucho" was propped up at the Chickering piano. This difficult piece of sheet music required my left and right hands to move in completely different directions and left me counting down the minutes until the end of the required daily hour of my musical suffering.

My father, sensing my dissatisfaction, suggested that he and I go into the city to hear the man he described as the "best piano player in the world." I was eight, and my father and I would be going to a nightclub together! I'd have him all to myself, a Freudian dream come true. I put on my most grown-up pleated skirt and saddle shoes, and we drove off, my father in the role of Dick Powell and I, his devoted and adoring June Allyson.

We sat at a small table in the dark, crowded room, my legs crossed in the sophisticated cocktail-party pose as my dad explained that the most thrilling thing about jazz was that the musicians were making nearly everything up right in front of us. There was a little bit they practiced, he said, but mostly they were doing what he reverentially described as improvising. I already knew that the classical music my mother listened to had every note already written down, and all the members of the orchestra were required to play them exactly as they were on the page—including the notations for loud or soft, fast or slow, no changes permitted. I decided then and there to grow up to become an adult who did what my dad admired. I'd improvise my life.

My thirteenth summer concluded with me several inches taller than I had been at its start and ominously approaching six feet. There were only two boys in my class that were taller than I was. I didn't like them, and they most decidedly didn't like me. In that way. And to make matters even more socially complicated, even if I were invited to a dance by a boy that was tall enough, I scorned the currently popular teen music.

Once a week, I tucked my allowance into my pocket and rode the bus to a record store with individual soundproof booths with turntables. Instead of Snooky Lanson and *Your Hit Parade* pop music that my father repeatedly belittled as not music at all, I'd listen to the most recent release from the Clovers, Ruth Brown, or Dinah Washington before deciding which one to buy, then return home clutching my new seventy-eight in its heavy paper sleeve and descend the basement steps into a dim, cluttered room filled with unused and broken castoffs, but perfect for dreaming.

With a mirror propped up against the back wall, I listened to Nat King Cole and the Platters, holding a broom as I spun and swirled with the tall boys who swept me into the effortless dips and backbends I'd seen Cyd Charisse and Ginger Rogers perform in the movies. I was white and popular. Alternately, I sang, the broom as my microphone, transformed into Sarah Vaughan. People applauded and begged me for encores after each tune, as I bowed and smiled with modesty and pride in the dusty mirror. I was Black and famous. I was improvising.

TWO

At nineteen, I was both married and a mother. In 1960, the conventional forms of being a wife and the daily, hourly, second-by-second task of parenting were carefully scripted. But not for me. I would be a fun-loving and playful mother and encourage my child to express her feelings, whatever they were. She would be allowed everything my more traditional upbringing denied me.

We built block cities, read books, explored the park,

and took trips to the airport to see the planes take off and land. She was entirely loveable in the mornings, but inevitably became querulous, dirty, and demanding by midafternoon. I began to sense that how I treated my daughter might not prove to be the path that would dramatically reveal to my mother how she should have mothered me. Or contribute to my being seen, treated, and respected as an adult by her. My improvisation needed work.

Throughout my second pregnancy, I read psychology books about sibling relationships and how a firstborn might respond when another child joins the family. I wanted to grow our family thoughtfully, give my daughter a running start at sisterhood, one that had not been available to me. The child-rearing experts I consulted emphasized the ways an older child might feel displaced, jealous, competitive, or angry about the new baby, and how it was best to help them identify with the mother, not the baby. Not ever having access to my feelings about my brother's entrance into the family, whatever they were, I took this as gospel.

I bought a Popeye punching bag that was as tall as my now three-year-old daughter and the site, I carefully explained, where she could express all her feelings. She could yell at it, kick it, hit it. Ignore it. Whatever you're feeling, I concluded proudly. I bought a baby doll with a changing table and crib just for her. We were going to be two mommies together. Two big girls.

Everything went smoothly for the first few days after my return from the hospital. We bathed our babies, dressed them, fed them, talked to them. But all that carefully curated serenity evaporated on the day she abruptly turned away from her rubber charge floating in the watery plastic tub, leaving her to drown, walked over to the punching bag, and delivered a few desultory pokes. She turned and looked at me, slapped at the bag once more, then marched over and firmly hit me. As hard as a three-year-old could.

Having already promised myself that I would never, ever, under any circumstances yell at my child, with studied calm I murmured, "Why did you hit Mommy, sweetheart? That's why Popeye is there. So you can have your feelings with him."

She stood, legs planted firmly apart, stared at me, and said, "But I'm not mad at Popeye, Mommy. I'm mad at you. I want you to take this baby back where you got her. Right now."

I was proud of her. She knew how she felt and was expressing herself. I was also relieved that her father wasn't home, aware that his response wouldn't have been nearly so sanguine. This improvising business was going to be more complicated than I had thought.

As my daughters got older, I introduced feeling words into our conversations to help them build up a vocabulary of identifiers. Shy. Nervous. Confused. I found teaching moments everywhere, even when they were simply telling me what happened at school. They were patient with my eager efforts at eliciting their real feelings. But as they were broadening their emotional range, so was I. Restless. Trapped. Anxious.

I was in my twenties and at the tail end of a marriage that had gone on too long. When the girls were in school, I went to visit the museum of art and sit in the garden in front of a Gaston Lachaise statue. I was drawn to her, a massive bronze figure, hands on her hips, muscular shoulders and legs, hair contained in a bun, commanding the space in the garden, other sculptures and visitors dwarfed by her presence.

She was what I wanted to become. A big woman. I wanted to stand, legs apart, hands on hips, gaze steady, a force in my own life. I also wanted to touch her body and daydreamed about approaching her and gently sliding out the pins that held her bun in place, allowing her hair to come undone and cascade down her back, and then burying my hands in it. I scared myself with those thoughts, imagining people could see into my mind and know what I was thinking. What I was wanting. To look like her. To make love to her. To become her.

But what came undone as America moved more deeply into the 1960s and the world shifted in ways that drew me toward it and away from family was me. I wanted to join people my own age, unencumbered by husbands and children, who were beginning to resist the authorities of government, schools, and laws that shaped and defined American life.

I, like my mother before me, had unwittingly become trapped in a too-small world of husband and children. Home and garden. Errands and entertaining. My home, like hers, was filled with objects, taking on a life of its own. I moved in smaller and smaller circles. From the stove to the table. From the carpool to the market. Shepherding my daughters to friends' houses to play in their well-equipped backyards.

I couldn't improvise on my life as it was. I had to leave it behind, turn the page to see what was next. And without understanding the consequences of that decision, I did.

THREE

When my mother was eighty-three, she arrived to celebrate her birthday, careful to be attentive to my rhythms as I am when visiting my daughters. I brought her a cup of coffee as she pretended to be reading, but I knew she was waiting for me to join her, this old woman who held so tightly to the certainties she labored so hard to learn. The right and wrong ways to live, to think, to act, to dress, to be a woman. All the notes as written.

We began our conversation, as we often did, talking about the recent death of an old friend, another loss in her shrinking world. I told her that death is an ongoing part of my life as well, the breast cancer and AIDS epidemics ending any notion that death is the province of the old. I talked about some of the ways people are creating ethical wills, family videos, oral histories— inviting the person who is coming to the end of their life to tell stories and remember what was most significant to them. And after their death, there are newly imagined ceremonies of mourning. My mother and I had never spoken of her death. She'd simply said that her "wishes" were in the safe deposit box and that she expected I'll follow them to the letter.

"What do you mean?" she asked, puzzled. "How can you make up a ceremony?"

I described the day when my friends and I had created our own Yizkor ritual, a part of the Yom Kippur service during which Jews honor their dead. Nine of us gathered in a living room to elaborate on the traditional form, remaking it into a time both to remember the lives of our ancestors and to identify and release any regrets about our choices in the past year. We were a circle of Jewish American women, all feminists, some secular and political, others with a Jewish practice, expanding, deepening, improvising what we needed.

"But how can you do that?" my mother interrupted. "Prayers are supposed to be the way they're written, the way they have been done for centuries. You just can't call yourself a Jew and make it up. There's a right way to do things. An appropriate way."

"Appropriate" provided the template for a girl of the 1940s. There were appropriate ways to sit and eat, to talk and dress, to catch a ball and talk to a grown-up. Appropriate ways even to pray.

"And that's not all. Your need to talk about everything is something I don't understand. I'm a private person. I know what I feel, but I don't need to say it out loud to another person. I could never do what you do."

Stung, I answered sharply, "Ma, it isn't necessary to compare everything. I'm just telling you the ways we are starting to reimagine rituals. Your way is different. Not better. Just different."

She continued pensively, as if I hadn't spoken, as if I weren't even in the room with her.

"I remember when Momma died. I couldn't even sit there while they were doing what they pretended was sitting shiva. What they were doing was having a party. There were big platters of food and people stuffing their faces like they had never eaten before. Laughing, talking. As if my mother wasn't dead. Being there made me feel even more lonesome. I wanted to be quiet in my own house to mourn for my mother."

"I know, Ma, but some women find that talking about the person who has died makes them feel better, closer to the person. Can't it just be that you don't like it? That you never wanted to do it? Not that people who do it are wrong?"

As I impatiently put down my coffee cup, she began to weep.

"Maybe I'm talking about me. I wonder what will happen when I die. Are you going to sit with your friends and talk about me? Tell things about me? I think that my life would have been different if I could verbalize how I'm feeling the way you do. I just can't do it. Something inside me can't. It's just a different time. Nowadays, women talk about things we never did. Maybe, if I had been able to, I wouldn't have kept so much inside myself." She settled heavily in the chair and blew her nose in the napkin, signaling an end to the conversation.

Later, as she was preparing for bed, she said, "When I'm gone, you're the only one I'll miss."

Frightened and trying to lighten the moment, I replied, "How can you miss me if you're gone?"

"I make up a story," she said. "Doesn't everybody make up a story they can believe in?"

"Yes, Ma, they do," I said, taking her in my arms. "They make it up."

FOUR

After she died, I was left with stories that I was finally old enough to understand. Stories about my mother's hungers for me and disappointments for herself. Stories about my urgency to create a different kind of life, only to discover all roads led back to her. Stories about how I had mothered and who I was becoming as an old woman.

Over my desk is a faded three-by-five card in the handwriting of my beloved, now dead for thirty-three years. During the last month of her life, she wrote, "There is no greater gift than that of the new day," and pinned it up on the wall by her sickbed. After her death, I framed the note and hung it above my desk. I read it each morning and remind myself that I'm about to receive a gift. She is the woman who, my youngest daughter observed, taught me how to play; I, such an earnest political activist when we met, and she like quicksilver.

Early in our courtship, we were picnicking at a park on a high, grassy incline that leveled off alongside a children's playground.

"I wonder what it would be like to roll down this hill," she teasingly suggested.

"Not me," I smilingly and I hoped successfully demurred.

"Come on. It will be fun. Like skiing but with our whole bodies!"

"I'm too tall to do something like that," I said, offering the only rejoinder I could.

Those words were my mother's, who had always cautioned me not to wear vertical stripes because they accentuated my height. Not to talk too loudly or with my hands or eat with my fingers. Never to draw attention to myself in those ways. Her lifelong admonishments precluded any possibility of me being the kind of woman who rolled down hills.

But she was already lying down and, looking up at me with great confidence, said, "See you at the bottom, love."

And off she went.

I was already in love with this woman, now halfway down the hill, and there was nothing for me to do but anxiously push off. During that exhilarating tumble in Dolores Park in 1978, my mother's anxious guidance began to dissolve, and left in the space her protective worries had filled were the beginnings of an exuberance and un-self-consciousness I hadn't imagined possible. Certainly not for such a tall, dedicated, and solemn woman as I.

Now, when the doctor suggests I use hiking poles to take the weight off my ruined knee, each walk takes me to another part of the world. The frontage road outside my apartment house has become the portal to international travel with my poles serving as my magic carpet. I become an intrepid adventurer. I hear my lover's voice urging me toward splendid landlocked adventures. Mondays I trek in Nepal. Thursdays I meander in the Cotswolds, Friday is always a safari. I improvise.

FIVE

I'm so much braver now that time is running out. I don't have time to mess around with things that don't matter. I wish I had figured that out earlier, but there is something about the urgency of time passing that has turned out to be supremely motivating. There is no greater gift than that of the new day. And I want each day to be as improvisational as I can make it. I've gotten really good at it. I've been practicing for decades.

MY QUIXOTIC HAIL-MARY PASS

When I was about to turn seventy, I was aware that while it wasn't the end of the world or even of my life, it meant I was old. Not really, really old, but *oldish*.

After listening to my typically melancholy musings about the pleasure and difficulty of this milestone, a woman I have known for decades told me, "It's time you broadened your horizons." I waited for her to go on, but she just looked at me expectantly.

Squaring my shoulders, I replied, "What's wrong with my horizons? I like my horizons just as they are, thank you." When she didn't answer, I asked, "What exactly are you talking about? Do you want me to learn to tap dance or something?"

"You need to start dating," she replied firmly.

"We're changing the subject right now," I said, "and I'm not kidding."

But later that same evening, I began to wonder if my friend might be right: I had been single for many years, and even though I liked living this way, a change might be interesting. I decided I'd check out the internet dating sites. Why not?

At the time, I found that while all the singles sites were somewhat different, there was a template for the process. First you had to click the links that defined who you were and what kind of person you wanted. These are called the deal breakers.

What were my deal breakers? Well, I wanted to meet a woman. I didn't want her to be a smoker. Not cigarettes, anyhow. She had to be well educated and leftist in her politics. I wanted her to be within a fifty-mile radius. I began to worry that the deal breakers were getting too numerous. And I wasn't in a position to be so categorical; there weren't that many seventy-somethings looking for love online.

My categories grew even longer. I didn't want to live together. One woman seemed like a match except that when I scrolled through her profile, she turned out to be five feet two inches tall. I am five feet ten (I used to be six feet but seem to be shrinking). It appeared I wasn't flexible about much. I reviewed my categories. Ethnicity. I checked "don't care." Hair, eyes, body type, "don't care." Religion, "don't care." Actually, I did care but decided to wait and see. Could I even imagine having a relationship with a religious fundamentalist? Would a fundamentalist want to have a relationship with me, a cranky, political Jew?

Some of the sites had tests that told you what kind of person you are. They required comparing shapes and other Rorschachian tests. I emerged from that visual gauntlet defined as a negotiator/innovator. *Like the weekly horoscope,* I thought, *well . . . maybe.* But I liked being identified that way. It took some of the sting out of all my deal-breaker categories and made me seem more flexible, openhearted, and fun loving than I was.

Joining four sites, I filled out personal profiles, making each a bit different since I figured they attracted different women. A little more intellectual emphasis in one. Political activism highlighted in another. A focus on my friendship community in a third.

Then I needed to choose a photograph. Some of the more expensive sites allowed multiple ones, but the choice of the primary image required clarity about how I wanted to be seen. Warm and smiling? Earnest and studious? At a political rally? At a celebration? At my desk? At a piano? Just a standard headshot with no context at all? I looked through all my available photographs, checking to see if my neck was wrinkled and if I had remembered to elevate my chin at the moment the flash went off. I settled on a standard smiling headshot, one with a moderately smooth neck. Then a second shot

of me sitting on the beach, happy, hair looking particularly good as it blew in the wind, although my breasts
seemed to be nestled somewhere near my waist since I
was wearing my beach bra, the really comfy, loose one.
I hesitated about the breast thing for a bit, and then
decided that the bodies—hers and mine—weren't that
important. That is, unless she was a foot shorter than
I was.

By then, I had read hundreds of profiles online to
get a sense of how women described themselves. Most
were crowded with descriptive adjectives, yet they
were completely opaque. Warm yet private. Outgoing
but needing solitude. Reader but loved to play games.
I settled on generic, warm, and only mildly truthful
language: I called myself a friendly political radical. A
warm disrupter of the state.

Several levels of suggested contact were part of the
process. After a woman saw your profile, she could
either (depending on the site) electronically wink or
smile at you. This expressed interest but didn't require
the interested person to make actual contact. On the
cheaper sites, one was able to ignore the winking and
smiling, but on the more costly ones, there was a link
that said "Thanks, but not interested." With higher fees
came a bit of courtesy.

Once my profile was online, I was winked and
smiled at dozens of times by a wide range of potential
matches. A European woman wanted to correspond.

A newly divorced woman sought someone to "gently bring her out." A woman in her late sixties spent two sentences of her allotted profile space assuring the viewer/reader that she looked younger than her years and preferred younger women as well. *Then why is she writing to me?* I wondered. Many of these winkers and smilers seemed too good to be true. How many people do you know who are playful, funny, intelligent, healthy, religious (or spiritual, a different category), and adventurous; love opera and country and western; and have recently taken up woodworking as a hobby?

I was beginning to suspect that I should revise my profile, just tell the truth, and save everyone concerned a lot of time. I'm, as I said before, a cranky, political Jew. I'm bossy, although I don't mean to be, and very opinionated. I don't really exercise four to five times a week, although each week I mean to. I make little exhalations each time I sit down and push down firmly against the chair seat when I rise. I wear hearing aids, and when they become loose, I poke my fingers into my ears and press them back in—which, if you don't know what I am doing, may look like a demented tic.

Next was the problem of figuring out where this hypothetical woman and I might meet. I no longer ordered salads in restaurants with people I didn't know because lettuce tucks itself away between my teeth and comes to rest there. I couldn't pick my teeth on a date. Then there was the added problem of the sound level of cafés. It would be very unromantic to keep interrupting with "What?" "Sorry, didn't hear you," or "Boy, it's loud in here." What with my periodontal pockets and the typical sound level, restaurants were not my first choice. Perhaps a walk would be better. But walking might mean something different to a prospective date than it did to me. It could be a Walk, involving hilly terrain, a good deal of speed, even sweating and grunting. Given the arthritis that had blossomed in my left knee and threatened to make significant inroads in my right one, I decided to omit this from my profile. Strolling along a flat surface would be OK. Sitting down in a quiet place and having a deep conversation would be the absolute best.

Soon after I got myself online, I saw a perfect woman, or at least one who was almost perfect. The right age, education, politics, even height. I thought, *This is easy. Why have I waited so long to enter the online world?* I sent what I thought was a warmly effusive email to this nearly perfect woman. Brief but charming, I imagined. After noting all our points of connection and interest, I proposed we meet for coffee. Pleased with myself and the alignment of the dating fairies, I waited for her response.

The first day I checked my email every couple of hours, the second day at fifteen-minute intervals. On the third day, I began to tell myself that this woman must have gone on an already-planned trip after she put her profile online. If she had seen my response before she left, she certainly would have been as delighted as I was to find her, and she would have responded at once. By the fourth day, the story changed: it was now about the callous and unkind person who had put her profile online and didn't even bother to respond, if she had only stopped to think about it, to a woman who was a good prospect. By the fifth day, I was beginning to suspect that this process was going to be more complicated than I had thought.

I was drowning in a sea of smiles and winks from all the wrong people. My response was to add a revised profile to a new site, hoping that the women there would be more . . . something.

I got a haircut (that drew attention up and away from my neck) and began to respond to the women who were interested in me. Each week I had a handful of breakfast dates—pancakes and eggs are not foods that stick in my teeth. One woman wanted a life partner right away. Another wanted to share her horse farm with the right woman. Another had just broken up from a twenty-year relationship and wanted to make new "friends," although the glint in her eye belied the "friendliness" of her interest. Another was an old hippie. Then an ardent (read rigid) Marxist.

Driving home from these breakfasts where I inevitably overate, I tried to invoke my spiritual practice, wavering though it was. *Be compassionate to yourself,*

I silently intoned, *and to each of these women reaching out for love. Be patient, loving, openhearted, and kind in your assessment of them, yourself, and this process. Repeat five times and breathe.*

Who knows? I thought. *Maybe when I get home and open my web browser, there will be a smile or a wink from the right, even the perfect, woman.*

DOWN THERE

I haven't had a lover in several decades and no longer require one in order to have an entirely satisfying sexual life. My right hand has become my in-house companion. There is no longer any need for conversation, a glass of wine before, or coffee the following morning.

There are moments when, unexpectedly, I'm filled with appreciation for my body, remembering all the places it's been and adventures it's had, and I want to make love to it. As a thank you. I take my time and do a thorough top-to-toe job. This doesn't involve, as it might for some, creating a mood. I don't light candles or find just the right music for the moment. Even when I was younger, I was never drawn to the predictable accoutrements of a sexual encounter, preferring stimulating conversation over glasses of wine, eventually shifting from minds to bodies, happy to skip all the extraneous artifacts. First, because every time I had sex was not necessarily romantic, and second, even if it were, the candles might tip over and burn everything down. Music, unless it was almost too soft to be heard, would preclude any conversation the two of us might want to have. My hearing began to decline precipitously in my forties, and tender murmurs during sex, if there was music playing in the background, would have required me to either pretend I'd heard and appreciated what I presumed was a random endearment, or break whatever the mood was entirely and whisper back, "What?"

My reasons for wanting to have sex with another person have varied widely over my lifetime. Sometimes I felt desire for them. At other times, I wanted to be desired by them. These are not at all the same thing, but ideally related. There were times when having sex seemed like a good idea because the relationship had become stale and our bodies might help us rediscover what we once had. Or reveal what we no longer did. There was curious sex, the eyes meeting across a crowded room thing. Lonely sex, just wanting another 98.6-degree creature beside me in the night. Predictable sex, which emerged after learning one another's bodies over time. This could be a comfort or an irritation, depending on the moment. There was playful and casual sex after an evening of good talk and energetic dancing. Interludes that might have gone somewhere but didn't. I haven't missed much in the sex department.

Now that I am in a primary and entirely monogamous relationship with myself, I've considered opportunities to enhance my pleasure and researched the latex and plastic devices that augment the sex lives of some of my women friends, and from what I understand, millions of others.

In the past, sex toys were an occasional and very peripheral aspect of my sexual life. Recently, wanting to keep things imaginative and expansive, I responded to an ad for a vibrator that had several appendages designed to pleasure my body in multiple ways at once. Batteries included. I told myself not to make up my mind in advance about inserting more than one appendage into my body and ordered one. In purple.

When it arrived, carefully packaged in the kind of plastic you need pliers to open, it seemed huge. Certainly bigger than where it needed to go. I wasn't sure how to make all the supplemental additions work at the same time, was distracted by the irritating buzzing the battery power pack made, and after nearly a dozen attempts to experience multiple pleasures from multiple protuberances, I gave up. My right hand is the right size, doesn't buzz, and needs no batteries.

Then there is pornography, which mostly men and, I know, some women use for fantasy sex. I know both porn and attitudes about it have changed a lot over the past decades, and there are women creating videos designed to illuminate a mutual experience. But when I try to watch them, I'm not able to get past the women's eyes. They look empty. Blank. I scan their faces as they go through their carefully choreographed motions, trying to imagine their lives, perhaps the children they are trying to raise, the money they are trying to save to get a new start, the poor choices that got them out of their abusive homes but only as far as this video. Sometimes porn makes me outraged as well, but it always makes me sad. Sorrow doesn't lend itself to either arousal or fantasy. Not for me. I guess that makes me old school.

I depend on my own imagination, which is well developed. I've become practiced at this, writing the scenario of the moment in my mind, then casting the actor or actors to fulfill the story line. Everyone's limbs are flexible and sinuous; no one has a rotator-cuff limitation or gets a cramp at a moment that doesn't lend itself to cramping. There are never walls to bang up against, skin doesn't get pinched by mistake, positions shift with grace, and nothing ungainly ever occurs. It's like an endlessly pleasurable ballet in which I am always—*always*—the star. All the pleasure is designed and experienced by me. No relating needed. It's not that I don't enjoy relating. I have decades-long friendships with women, and I relate all over the place with them. Sex for me now is simply and only about pleasure. Mine.

My body continues to let me know when such pleasure would be welcome. My "down there," as I have tenderly called it since the early days of second-wave feminism, sends up an alert. A tingle. Sometimes a series of flutters. The message is always the same. Pay attention to me, please. I'm down here alone and unattended. Of course, if I'm having lunch with a friend, at the movies, or driving the car, I can't simply stop and attend. Nevertheless, I do take those fluttering messages seriously and with the same focused attention I once brought to my lovers. But now, I have to factor in the time of day because I learned as a young woman that all too often upon reaching orgasm, sometimes in the next breath, I'm asleep. That ends the possibility of tender postcoital exchanges, which was problematic when I was having sex with people who wanted to talk, scramble an egg, or cuddle afterward. Now, when I need to get to sleep, sex with myself is better than Ambien. Much, much better. I wait until as late in the day as possible because of the falling-asleep thing and sink into a happy and satisfied slumber, one I've provided for myself.

Now my sexual life is guaranteed to be exactly what and when I want and need. Because I'm the lover and the lovee. The flow of communication between us is unspoken but immediately clear. Here. Not there. Pause. Recommence. I've become the perfect sexual partner, with a deeply appreciative audience of one.

FULL-BODY SCAN

As I drove down the freeway earlier today, my radio program was interrupted by an enthusiastic young man suggesting products I might buy to overcome the ravages of the aging process. *Really?* I thought. *Am I ravaged? Ravaged* sounded permanent. Like a building that had already collapsed.

Since arriving home, I've removed my coat and shoes, then my bra (we'll get to that later), and readied myself for a full-body scan to assess my ravages. Pulling off my socks, I focus on a nearly forty-year-old bunion (a direct consequence of the requisite pointed-toe shoe designs of my prefeminist young adulthood), covered with a day-old curling bunion pad, and start the process at ground level.

My feet are decidedly flat. When I was eight years old, my anxious mother took me to a chiropodist who determined that I needed steel arch supports placed inside my Buster Brown oxfords. They didn't work, my arches never rose, and he later became my piano teacher, but that's another story. My toenails are currently a bright red because five of my old woman friends and I just came back from a vacation/celebration of our thirty-year friendship, and knowing I would be wearing a bathing suit in public, I had decided to paint the parts of my body that still lent themselves to decorative enhancement.

Moving northward, I arrive at two silvery scars, one over each knee, announcing the placement of titanium where there once was bone. I could have paused to mention puffy ankles from middle-aged falls that I never bothered to treat. I just elevated, iced, and forgot about them. I still do. My ankles are functional. Strangers pat my knees every time I go through an airport screening, but they work remarkably well. The pain of the surgery has dimmed just as my surgeon— who had a blindingly toothy male smile—assured me it would: "It's like childbirth." *How the fuck do you know what childbirth is like?* I thought. But he was going to be redesigning my body with complex carpentry, and I was going to be unconscious. It didn't seem the moment for feminist education.

Then there are my thighs, puffy like my ankles. I have hated them since I was a teenager. Of course, they were probably lovely sixty-eight years ago, but in those critical years, when the desire for bodily perfection was at its height, I was certain that my thighs were all wrong and too thick because their insides rubbed together when I walked. I didn't want them to touch, but no matter what I did, including wearing a girdle for a painful year, they continued to touch and still, all these decades later, make insistent and ongoing daily contact.

Right at the juncture of those unsatisfying thighs is my pudenda, now oddly girlish, exposed and with dandelion-like puffs of gray, all that remains of my once-full, dark, and curly pubic hair.

Moving around to my buttocks, which are heeding the inevitable call of gravity and inching ever southward, I come upon folds and creases, my skin undulating and softening. Viewed through a more astrophysical lens, my behind resembles the pockmarked surface of the moon.

Then there is my stomach. It has done herculean (Megaranic? She was Herc's first wife.) service over my lifetime. Both my now-middle-aged daughters got their start in there. It was a home, a sanctuary, a hatchery. Now it's a fallen soufflé.

My breasts have always been large and over the decades have become increasingly pendulous, requiring a bra with a sturdy wire to hold them still. I had a period of bra experimentation during my sixties, searching to find just enough wire to hold me up with just enough elastic to keep everything in place, and my second drawer (the first is for underpants and the third for socks) is filled with an assortment of my efforts to find the right band, size, and shape. As a result, I have no bras that fit me comfortably in all ways, but some are better for sweaters, others for exercise, others for when I want to feel cute. I have lace, cotton, solids, patterns, and they all work to hold my breasts somewhere north of my stomach.

When I arrive home at the end of my day, the third thing I do, after removing my coat and shoes, is unhook my bra. The comfort of releasing my breasts from their daylong bondage and feeling them rest upon my chest and move around when I do is a great release and freedom, although not a freedom I am prepared to impose on the outside world.

I feel tenderly toward my breasts. I loved a woman who had cancer and had one breast removed, and I know how much she missed it/her (we had named them) until she died three years later. I'm grateful to have been able to keep my own shapeless bundles.

My arms are currently decorated in deep purple splotches, which are the combined result of having thin skin (both physically and emotionally) that bruises at the slightest provocation and the side effect of a medication (one of many) I am taking for rheumatoid arthritis. The bruises begin with small, randomly patterned rose-colored spots that mysteriously expand, assuming amoeba-like designs on my arms, becoming a glowing deep purple, eventually fading, only to reform with small spots in another location. Like a light show.

The skin of my underarms waves like seaweed when I move. My fingernails split and crack easily. I've rubbed vitamin E into them every day for fifteen years, which so far does not appear to have slowed the tempo of their decline, but has left vitamin E stains on many of my sleep T-shirts.

Moving northward I come to my neck, which, compared to some necks, is pretty OK. No wattles. No deep jowls. Just an ordinary eighty-three-year-old's number of wrinkles. I know a woman who had a face-lift, which left her face as smooth as a baby's behind but connected to an old woman's crinkly neck.

We arrive at my face, which, during the past twenty years, has sprouted deep grooves, apparently while I slept, like tributaries that ought to lead to some central channel but instead meander across my cheeks, around my eyes and mouth. A face full of channels, leading nowhere. Liver spots of a variety of sizes and shades mark the spaces between.

Once, my middle-aged daughters, who were in the process of figuring out their own middle-agedness and not entirely comfortable being confronted with such an old mother, took me to Sephora where we all bought products, leaving with a bag stuffed full of brushes, emollients, and creams designed to put an abrupt and permanent end to aging. I made one failed effort at exfoliating, plucking, moisturizing, concealing, and blushing. My tributaries and liver spots remained, but my skin looked glittery, like I was perspiring in a different color. Still, I can't bring myself to throw all the stuff out, and the remains of my efforts are in a plastic bag under my bathroom sink next to the economy-size bag of cough drops.

My teeth appear to be holding on, although when I smile broadly, which I often do, one has a bird's-eye view of the archeology of my dental life. The white part of my smile is in the front. Moving to the sides and back, one sees a repository of old silver fillings, aging gold crowns, and a bridge that is increasingly wobbly. But the front, except for one tooth that appears to be sliding sideways, has the help of whitening strips I use every few months. The theory is that being blinded by the whiteness of the front of my mouth will keep eyes averted from the silver and gold glistening from within its recesses.

My ears are plugged with aids without which I can only smile warmly, read the lips of the speaker, and try to respond in a way that has some relationship to what is said. I began wearing hearing aids nearly half a lifetime ago when my love was dying. After multiple and unsuccessful efforts at encouraging me to see an audiologist, which I repeatedly and determinedly assured her I didn't need to do, she asked, "But, honey, what if I'm on my deathbed and want to say a deeply important thing to you, and you can't hear me?"

That did it. I had a hearing-aid exam the very next day, not wanting to miss what might be her whispered deathbed wisdom, which turned out to be a wordless and very tender smile. I began with one "skin-colored," peanut-size apparatus, deciding to start with only one ugly appliance at a time. But while driving home I heard a fire engine approaching and couldn't tell whether it was behind me or approaching from the side. I relented and purchased the second one. Over the years they have become smaller and more accurate. Now they're just an automatic part of starting my day.

My eyes have been covered by glasses since before I entered middle age, but now I try to purchase stylish and colorful designs, given that there is little remaining style or color in my face. Just those tributaries and liver spots. For the past ten years, my glasses have been a bright red. I wear earrings to add something decorative to my face, although in truth, when I'm having a conversation with someone, I want them to be looking at my face, not my ears.

Ah, but then there is my hair. I have glorious gray, thick, wavy hair. There is the inevitable thinning spot at the crown—everyone has that, my hairdresser reassuringly tells me—but my hair has been a source of pride since my ponytail days, and on through the pixie, the bouffant, the butch spikes, the long and flowing, and the arranged to appear not arranged. Stylish, I think, and quite beautiful.

When I was in my forties, my life centered on what my mother resignedly called "rabble-rousing" and what my daughter called, when her teacher asked her what her mother did, "hectoring people." I was a rabble-rousing hectorer. I suggested to women that they go into their bedrooms, lock the door so they are assured they are alone, remove all their clothes, and stand in front of the mirror. Then, I would add, "See whose eyes you are looking through when you look at yourself. Are they your own or are they male eyes?'" Radical feminist hectorers understood the ubiquitousness of the male gaze and how most of us saw our bodies as never enough, too big, too small, too thick, too thin, wrong in every possible way. Always wrong.

I practiced my own exercise then and looked at my forty-five-year-old body with delight. I was sexual, I was strong, I was intact and healthy. I was certain that the eyes through which I was looking were my own. Except of course for the thighs. I skipped over them.

Now I repeat my own exercise, seeing the fleshy consequences of eighty-three years and all that I have asked of this increasingly exhausted vessel, all it has allowed me to do. Now my skin is old, softening, dry, wrinkled, and tired. I gently rub lotion over it with love.

ME AND AVA GARDNER

In the heart of the French village where I'm vacationing is a boutique owned by a Parisian who sells her designer clothing here during the summer. She's a stately woman who commands everyone's attention, including mine, at the evening concerts in the town square, dressed in dramatic black-and-white geometric outfits, with short, spiky white hair accentuated with large earrings, in direct contrast to the villagers wearing light floral cotton shifts and the tourists in T-shirts blaring slogans.

It took two hesitant days for me to make my way to her showroom filled with one-of-a-kind garments and designer jewelry. Everything was black, gray, ivory, taupe, and oatmeal. Not a color in sight. Racks of sleeveless dresses, snug on top with bell-shaped skirts filled with bold designs, lined one wall. I knew those wouldn't work, given that my upper arms are as dramatic in their own way as her clothes, but with more colorful designs—random purple dots punctuated by larger splotches. They're the result of both my teen years at the beach, one leg slightly raised and bent (cover-girl style) in an effort to glamorously tan, and my current and ongoing medications. The aftereffects of both now blossom in purpuras, amoeba-like up and down my old white senior arms.

Moving past the glorious but extremity-exposing dresses, I tried on a black linen tunic with cream borders and sleeves that flowed down my arms and draped around my body as though it had been created to live there. Of course, there was my deeply lined face and gray hair sticking out at the top and rubber-soled sneakers designed for my fear of twisting an ankle on the cobblestones so far from home at the bottom, but from neck to ankles, I was certain this was exactly what Ava Gardner would have chosen if she were still alive and in this shop.

I had read everything about her early marriages to Mickey Rooney, which I didn't understand, and Artie Shaw, which I certainly did. I knew that she repeatedly fought and made up with Frank Sinatra, had exuberant affairs with bullfighters, and danced in the street. She was sultry and tempestuous, which I hoped one day to become. Alone in my bedroom, I unfastened the elastic band that held my ponytail, practiced tossing my hair as she did, and worked on my come-hither smile that I hoped would eventually be put to successful use.

I left home in much the same way Ava did, racing into and out of an ill-fated first marriage. But with no Artie Shaw to rescue me, I was left to my own devices. Fashion had changed, and Veruschka, a model even taller than I, was on magazine covers and had become my new template for how to dress. Now, everything I wore was black, my turtleneck sweaters and jeans augmented with hammered-silver earrings and necklaces, my long hair no longer in a ponytail but curled like hers, set each night with empty frozen-orange-juice cans, to appear as though it naturally cascaded down my face and shoulders. It was hard to sleep with cans on my head, but that was the price I was willing to pay. My eyes were outlined with dark liner, creating, I hoped, an internationally cosmopolitan look. Elizabeth Taylor had just filmed *Cleopatra*, and even nice Jewish girls were trying to look Egyptian.

My carefully curated presentation was augmented by a book, usually Camus, Rilke, or Lorca, identifying me as a bohemian kind of intellectual, someone a smart and free-spirited guy would want to approach. And maybe date. But the succession of self-identified free spirits I met turned out to be neither smart nor free spirited. After the evening when, over spaghetti and meatballs, I was the recipient of an impassioned interpretation of *The Faerie Queene*'s relationship to colonialism, I relievedly pulled my hair back into a ponytail, allowing myself the ability to have a good night's sleep. I wasn't going to have Veruschka's life and certainly not Ava's, so I returned to the more pressing task of trying to figure out my own.

The beginnings of my lifelong sartorial restraint were the result of a spurt of growth at thirteen running out of pituitary steam only when I reached the full and alarming height of six feet. There was one other girl in my eighth-grade class as tall as I was who slumped when she walked through the halls. After observing her for a few days, I concluded that her efforts at diminishing herself left her looking hunched over, but every inch as tall. If I was going to be an outcast forever, which I was sure would be the direction of my future, I could at least look like a proud outcast who stood up straight and didn't care at all that everyone was secretly laughing at me. Seventy years later, I still have the best posture of every one of my friends.

Once or twice a month, I'd return from school to discover a dress or skirt with the tags still on it draped across my bed. My mother had gone to Lane Bryant, the only clothing store in Boston for "big women," but still nothing for "tall" or for "girls" in 1952, and scoured its racks for clothes that would fit me and most resemble whatever was currently in style. It took decades for me to appreciate the kindness those offerings represented, how she was trying to protect me from the humiliation of being thirteen and having so few choices. But even with her efforts, their clothes assumed that anyone needing a size large would be an adult woman, not a teenage girl. And she would be wide, not tall. Even their smallest sizes were much too big, although the length of both sleeves and skirt was a polyester success.

Then there were shoes. My father was a salesman who sold leather goods to shoe factories, and whenever he returned from the regional shows with a duffle bag filled with size 4 sample shoes for my tiny cousin Ada, I hated her and her feet so much I couldn't breathe. I was already a flat-footed 10½, and while I looked like a stiffly held six-foot ruler topped with a ponytail and ending in orthopedic shoes, in my secret heart, I was Ava Gardner.

Twenty-five years ago, I impulsively bought a striking taffeta caftan with asymmetric silver buttons. Later, on a trip to the Southwest, fueled by the enthusiasm of friends, I got a three-quarter-length red cape with an attached scarf that presumably was designed to be flung around my neck. I was never quite sure how to carry off the flinging part. I've never figured it out with scarves either. I've even watched videos about how to appear like I just offhandedly, with a slight twist of my wrist, draped them chicly around my neck, but I always end up looking like I have a sore throat.

The cape was woolen and itchy, and the caftan was effused over by my daughter with such barely masked longing that I gave it to her. Those outfits represent the me I always intended to become but hadn't. The Ava me.

My ex-husband's third wife (I was his second) was a glamorous woman, and whenever there were family occasions, photo albums reveal my failed efforts at stylishness. She dyed her hair in that costly way where it doesn't look dyed although you know it has been, wore enormous necklaces intended to make their own statement, discovered designers before they became well known, and wore their sculptured dresses with boldness and confidence.

Pictures of both of my daughters' weddings illustrate the visual gulf between wife two and wife three. I always reined myself in well short of flamboyance. I look the way I've always looked. Earnest. I even smile earnestly.

Unable to find a sophisticated job that would allow me to wear fashionable clothing, I found more pedestrian work as the "'chairside girl'" in a downtown dental office. Five days a week for the next seven years, my daily wardrobe shifted from one that had been exclusively black to one that was now entirely white. Each morning I dressed in one of my three white starched nurses' uniforms, pulled on thick white stockings, and slid my feet into enormous white oxfords. My clothes were now as utilitarian as my life.

Eventually I returned to college in an adult degree program that offered evening classes for working students, developing dental x-rays by day and writing research papers by night. Jeans or a bathrobe replaced the black cocktail dresses that had gone the way of the Faerie Queen. On weekends, I wore whatever was on the chair beside the bed. Periodically, I'd replace what I had with more of the same. The requirements were that they be moderately priced, didn't require dry cleaning, and blended with everything else I already had.

I approached my fortieth birthday party and the celebration of my first book by uncharacteristically allowing myself the excess of an elegant, blue, full-length velvet dress. I wanted to make an entrance every bit as dramatic as the adolescent me had dreamed about, filled with the oohs and aahs I imagined Ava had received when she arrived at Hollywood premieres. That was to be my reward for a decade of such hard and focused work, I told myself as I arranged the necessary monthly payments for my purchase. I remember little about the party now, but every moment of my sweeping through the door and slowly making my way into the center of the gathering is still gratifyingly vivid.

The morning after, that celebratory once-in-a-lifetime garment was hung in a closet filled with a conventional assortment of corduroy and woolen pants, cotton shirts, and sweaters.

My impulse to look at least somewhat avant-garde-ish has evaporated, and with white office uniforms now thankfully a thing of the past, my clothing choices are organized around three basic categories. The first are those for every day. This requires pants with elasticized waists and neutral colors. The tops range from turtle-neck sweaters to summer blouses that don't need ironing. My ironing days are behind me. My sole decorative additions are earrings crafted by feminist jewelers, consisting of labrys, sisterhood signs, and an occasional abstract shape, perhaps one that represents vulvas. Or freedom. I am never sure.

The second are *shmattes* I only wear at home. Those are both my worn-out everyday clothes and the things that accidentally got mixed in with bright colors in the laundry while I was absentmindedly attending to something else and are now a blurry pastel. They include the still perfectly good burgundy tunic with a big oil splatter caused by trying to sauté scallops with the burner on too high and my white pants with the rust-colored amoeba-shaped pocket wherein the Hershey's Kiss melted.

Then there are, what were called in my formative years, dressy clothes. They require complementary earrings and shoes with straps. I don't wear them very often though. My mother was raised in a family where the purchase of a new dress was a once-or-twice-a-year event. Her older sister always wore her new outfit to school the next day while my mother carefully saved hers for special occasions. I'm like her in that way, as in so many others. Last year while on a trip to Scotland, I bought a splendid hand-embroidered blouse, a garment I knew even then I probably wouldn't ever wear. I simply don't have many special occasions anymore. Not that I don't have occasions. I do. But their specialness doesn't require a change of clothes. So, like my long-ago blue velvet dress, the blouse lives out its neglected life in the back of my closet, dazzling but unworn. I'm saving it.

My shoes serve the same purpose my Buster Browns once did, providing support for fallen arches, wobbly ankles, and now, the addition of titanium knees. There are choices in my size now that are beautiful, every bit as lovely as my cousin Ada's size 4 shoes once were, and patiently await their moment in the sun. I have two pairs of mildly voguish additions—one is red and the other silvery. I often imagine that one day I'll wear the red ones with jeans—like Hollywood ingenues do when they pretend for the camera that they're going shopping. Or like Ava might have worn to dinner with

Artie. But I don't. I wear neutral, undemanding clothes. The older I get, the looser they become.

Now, I stood in front of the mirror in the atelier in Lagrasse, gazing at myself in a resplendent tunic, my earnest face at the top, sensible sneakers at the bottom, and remembered that once, at forty, there was a moment when I was briefly Ava Gardner, wearing a glorious blue velvet gown and walking my own red carpet.

Thanking the elegant couturier, I walked carefully down the cobblestone streets to my house, my loose cotton pants and gauzy blouse the attire of an old woman who looks exactly like herself.

THE UPSIDE-DOWN THING

My earliest attempts at sylphdom began when I first saw *A Dance to Spring*, a Jules Feiffer line drawing in the *New Yorker*. I had been a gym-class failure and never thought that wearing comfortable clothing and working up a sweat would be a productive path to health and well-being for me. I wanted something more, well, maidenly, and found it in yoga.

My practice began when my daughters were approaching their teen years. I wanted to be a good example for them, so I stopped smoking, drinking, and eating red meat. How this was going to help them navigate their own unruly adolescence wasn't clear, but it was the best idea I could come up with. Our family's alternative menu consisted of massive amounts of brown rice and bulgur with assorted steamed vegetables and vast quantities of carrot juice enlivened with a sprig of parsley, and at the center of every meal was tofu in all its barely edible incarnations. I purchased a juicer, a steamer, and a compost canister, committed as I was to becoming a part of the cycle of life.

Yoga was newly popular in the West and required wearing comfortable clothes, although there was some intermittent sweating involved. There were classes offered everywhere and hundreds of yogis touting their qualifications in this newly lucrative landscape. Since most were recent graduates of venerable yoga centers, I chose the Integral Yoga Institute, a primary source of many of these eager instructors. They had a policy that none of the other burgeoning and trendy yoga opportunities multiplying all over the city offered; if you supervised the children of parents (mothers, of course) taking a class, then yours would be free. The system of socialist-ish barter allowed entry to everyone who wanted to study, which addressed my critique of the rise of yoga capitalism.

Two winding flights of stairs led to a spacious entry where a young woman serenely smiled (smiles were always serene); signed you in; and took your shoes, coats, backpacks, and other accoutrements of your external material life. I never met any of the other students because we were expected to be yogic-ly tranquil, not Westernly chatty. I was happy to enter that kind of space but would have welcomed carrot or beet juice with one of the members of my class afterward. But we arrived and departed in harmonious silence.

My body took to yoga right away. The combination of dance, exercise, calm, and the exotic smells of incense drew me. We began our gathering in repose and ended the same way. That was the meditative part. Reflecting pensively while lying down seemed a compelling spiritual practice to me.

My hearing was still relatively unimpaired in those years, so the teacher's murmurs that later became a problem seemed spiritually congruent. Spiritual people weren't energetic and loud. They murmured.

There were basic instructions. We were to be in an appreciative relationship with the specificity of our own bodies. They were our holy vessels after all. We were to notice where opening was easier and where we were holding. Holding was bad, although the word *bad* was never uttered. That would be entirely too negative. Holding was undesirable. That allowed the earnest student to reach for the desire to release. The goal, although we weren't to have them, was to expand, soften, and release. We were not to compare our holy vessel with any other, but as we moved from pose to pose, I peeked at the vessels on the mats alongside my own to see where they were holding and releasing, so I could evaluate how I was doing. My assessment of the other students, or at least as many as I was able to observe without craning my neck, thus revealing my inability to remain entirely within, suggested I was excellent in some parts of my body—mostly my legs and hips. (They continue fifty years later to be my most flexible appendages.) I appeared to be only moderately successful with upper-body strength, much as was the case in grammar school when I tried and failed to climb the ropes in gym class. When we were guided into poses that required pushing down with our arms, my liftoff was negligible. Which continues to be the case.

Then there was the upside-down thing. When the practice focused on inversions, my budding yogic self-esteem plummeted. We were invited (poses were "invited," which made everything seem more collaborative, I suppose) to inhale, press down, and elevate our legs into a triumphant headstand. But even when my neck was safely cosseted in a padded form designed to hold me steady, the final attempt at inverting my body resulted in an apologetic downward thud and shamefaced commitment to try again during the next class.

Once, the teacher stood behind me and held my legs up so I could have the experience of being upside down. I hated it. *This is not normal,* I thought. *My blood is rushing all throughout my body in the wrong direction. I can't see anything. What's good about this?*

I have, over the years, tried other forms of exercise. I found an instructor who led a class predicated on the assumption that bodies were essentially Silly Putty and stretching every part of oneself far enough would reshape the fundamental contours of one's physical structure. That was an immediate failure. Zumba was fun musically, but there was the hot, sticky, sweaty thing. Tai Chi went way past serene, into interminable slow motion. I have even used machines in gyms designed to perfect specific parts of my body, until I concluded I didn't really care about having muscles. And there were too many people wearing comfortable clothing and sweating all around me.

I always return to yoga. I place my purple mat and two blocks on my living room rug, and off I go, through the series of poses I can still manage. Once I could sit, soles of my feet pressed against each other, and invite my knees to fall open and onto the floor. Now, I still sit and press my feet together but end up in a stubborn V shape, no longer a graceful unfolding flower. Child's pose was another failure. My knees simply wouldn't bend sufficiently for me to settle back on my heels. I always wobbled just above them, requiring a prop to close the distance. And now, decades later with two titanium knees, it's entirely out of the question. Once, I could fling my arms to the sky (a dropped ceiling with fluorescent lights) without the current limitations of an arthritic shoulder. Now, when I need to scratch my shoulder blade, I use a wooden spoon from the container next to the stove. Once, I could flawlessly execute exuberant lunges. Now, any carefree abandon exacts a price. Beyond its capacity for delight, such fervor can result in the need for elevating, icing, and moaning softly. (That part is just to comfort myself. Making self-pitying sounds has always provided solace.)

I can no longer navigate the triangle, the forward bend, the backward bend, actually most of the bends. But I can touch my toes, keep a steady balance on one foot for upward of thirty seconds while extending my leg in a right angle to my body, hold most poses significantly longer, and, if I'm showing off to myself, sing along with the music, mostly Al Green, that accompanies me. I've decided that singing counts as serenity. I'm an old yogi now, which I suspect will transition into becoming a chair yogi, then inevitably end up as a bed yogi.

I try to match my breathing with each pose, except when I am adding something new to my routine. Then my tranquility or showing off my singing is replaced with grunts. Those bursts of decidedly unmusical sounds spoil the entire ambience of the project, so I don't introduce new poses as often as I should. I'm trying to get over myself.

I'm careful never to do any form of exercise anywhere in the vicinity of a mirror. The reasons are obvious. I can only imagine myself as the perpetual maiden in Feiffer's *A Dance to Spring* as long as there is no image of me to contradict the fantasy. I never ever look down at my upper arms when I'm leaning over in a downward dog, because my skin wrinkles up and joins the rest of my body reaching for the floor.

Instead, I close my eyes and let the music wash over me. I am a lissome sylph. I am dancing to spring.

DANCING IN MY CHAIR

We dance in my synagogue. We also pray and exalt; we mourn and bless. But in an increasing number of reconstructionist and renewal congregations like mine, we dance. Not me. But a lot of us.

The bima of my synagogue no longer contains an austere row of high-backed, velvet-cushioned chairs upon which the rabbi, cantor, and solemn elders—all men—sat; now there are guitars, ouds, djembes, sometimes even entire drum kits. When praise is offered, music fills the sanctuary, and middle-class, middle-aged Jews rise and dance with beaming faces and outstretched arms. This is not the synagogue of my childhood.

Seventy-five years ago, my family, members of the newly minted middle class, attended services in a building whose very architecture soared to unimaginable heights, like the promise of America to its aspiring Jewish immigrants. While not regular attendees, we always were there on the High Holy Days, wearing our best clothes—my mother displaying her mink stole, and I always in a brand-new outfit—as much to show other congregants how successful our lives were as to respect the importance of the holiday.

The rabbi's sermons left his prosperous congregants proud of living in what was understood to be the greatest country on earth, which allowed them to fulfill the mitzvah of planting trees to support our brothers and sisters who were founding the state of Israel. Music was provided by the deep and melodious voice of the cantor and our virtuous accompaniment, and the only movement involved was when the rabbi instructed, "Please turn to page 138 and rise." Dutifully, we rose. Now, service leaders (not only rabbis lead services now) suggest that we "rise in body or spirit," in consideration of those who are unable to stand. I don't know what those overlooked congregants did in my childhood. Invisible to the leadership, perhaps they stopped attending.

I was expected to grow up and eventually, but not too soon, marry a Jewish boy who was going somewhere—anywhere as long as it was up—live in a Jewish neighborhood, have children, and live a Jewish life. My parents eagerly discarded the accented speech, old-fashioned ways, and hand-me-down clothes that had marked their childhoods. They were dedicated to becoming the right kind of Jews. Not commies, slumlords, gamblers, or anyone who did anything that might publicly dishonor the Jewish people. Not someone who drew attention to themselves. Nevertheless, my eagerly upwardly mobile family ended up with children who represented all but the slumlord categories.

I married at eighteen, had two daughters, and within seven years was divorced, which brought both unwelcome attention and tremendous shame upon the family. My new life was not mirrored anywhere in the Jewish world of my childhood, where wives stayed at home to care for their husbands and raise their children, much as my mother and her mother before her had done.

My daughters and I joined one of the first demonstrations against the war in Vietnam in 1964. As we marched down New York City's Fifth Avenue, three hundred strong, my daughters kept their eyes straight ahead, pretending to be oblivious to the eggs, red paint, and jeers flung at them. They were both proud and frightened, the former all I noticed. I dragged them to church basements and union halls where they slept stretched out on folding chairs as I attended yet another meeting. We were in the business of remaking the world. The Jewish wife and mother I had been trained to become had transformed into the disruptive, drawing-attention-to-myself, commie-adjacent Jew my parents feared.

Years later, when my beloved was dying of breast cancer, we attended weekly services at a newly formed gay and lesbian synagogue whose sanctuary was the basketball court of a local gym, the rabbi's bima under the hoop. Those were the AIDS years, and the cavernous space was filled with men devoted to Jewish practice and prayers, even after having been disowned by their Orthodox families. My partner's glistening bald head generated knowing nods of welcome from the men with whom we gathered on Saturday mornings, their own bodies altered by the chemicals fruitlessly offered to sustain their lives for just a bit longer. This was a homecoming for them, a place that was welcoming, a community that had formed, in part, because they were dying. The rabbi, himself a young gay man, created an enclave for Jews who were outside mainstream life and suffering with realities not yet acknowledged by more conventional congregations. My partner and I met with the rabbi and immersed ourselves in an investigation of ethical wills, Jewish mourning rituals, and a post-Holocaust view of cremation. Then, after our months of study and deliberations, we planned her funeral.

. . .

My congregational life has changed in ways that would have been unrecognizable to my parents and would have horrified my grandparents. Women are rabbis. A lot of women. Services, while hewing to the ancient structure, have been reimagined, reconfiguring nearly every aspect of worship. There are times for meditation and chanting. New liturgical music was written to reflect the current realities of Jewish life as the twentieth century came to its close. Shabbat gatherings are full of song, exuberant movement circles, and individual expressionist dancing. But not for me. I sing quietly because my voice is far from melodious, but my dancing days ended with "I Heard It through the Grapevine." Not that I wouldn't dance if that were playing now, but it never is. So I don't dance. Except maybe a little bit in my chair. I never join the congregation's exuberant promenades and improvisations.

I know that a lot of contemporary synagogues are responding to the fair-enough criticism that Jewish prayer services are insufficiently embodied. Too much head and heart and not enough arms and legs. But my arms and legs can remain at rest while my mind and heart are soaring all over the place. No problem.

The more pressing issue for me is that whenever long periods of standing are required, particularly during the Amidah—the opportunity for the congregant to rise and, in a long silence, speak directly from their heart to God—I become light-headed. I don't understand the correlation between the Amidah and my sensation of low-blood-sugar weakness, but the former always seems to trigger the latter. I stand, wrap my tallit over my head, prepare to offer my personal words, and almost immediately get dizzy and eventually need to sit down. When the service leader instructs us to rise in body or spirit, I have begun to lean toward letting the spirit rise, rather than risk drawing attention to myself in the midst of the most prayerful part of the service by toppling to the floor. I lean forward, my arms on my knees; lower my head; and do my best to imagine that I'm either standing or imitating Rodin's sculpture *The Thinker.* Either lends gravitas to the experience.

Then there is the ongoing reality of my straining to hear. When the speaker is communicating something of great significance, rather than bellow like the rabbis of my childhood, their voice drops to a whisper, presumably to hold our rapt attention. What I hear is "And Jacob and Esau embraced and *murmur . . .*" Or "Close your eyes and let your thoughts settle. Let yourself *murmur.*" While I appreciate the drama of their vocal range, I want to hear their words as well. Even when I place myself in the center of the front row, if I'm unable to see the lips of the speaker, I'm left trying to piece together what I imagine they're saying.

I've had to give up a central part of the synagogue's offering, which is a meditative approach to practice, because once invited to close my eyes, I can no longer hear what the always-whispering instructor is saying. Why do they invite me? Isn't asking considered respectful enough? And why do they whisper? Do they intend to create a meditative mood? Even so, I'd be better able to meditatively respond to their directions if I knew what the directions were. Instead, I sit quietly, waiting for rustling sounds around me to know a transition is occurring, at which point I gratefully open my eyes. I've tried peeking at the teacher's lips, but that contradicts the very point of the process. Peeking and meditating are not activities that lend themselves to joint application.

Yet I gratefully acknowledge what this small, radical congregation of twenty-first-century Jews has provided me: Gifts more powerful than being able to hear. Or stand. Contemporary Judaism is fueled by questions and challenges that have allowed me to become a witness to and participant in the renewing of our tradition, a transformation of what study, prayer, communal life, and contemporary interpretation can be, even as the ancient words continue to link me through thousands of years of history.

After a lifetime of hollering, of drawing attention to myself—for justice, for liberation, for freedom, for Jewish values—I'm coming to rest not in the quiet of my parents' generation, embedded in an anxious desire to blend into an imagined melting pot, but with a readiness to enter this last period of my life in community with spinning, singing, exuberant Jews.

And I'll dance in my chair.

MY SUMMER VACATION

Despite all my years of yoga, I am not a flexible person. And only intermittently spontaneous. I prefer to identify the who, what, where, why, when, and how. I am also an old person whose need for a reassuring sense of where I'm going has become increasingly pointless because I can already see the big thing that's ahead of me. It's the end of me. I am caught somewhere between the historic comforts and the current futility of planning.

In the rainy winter season before the still-unimaginable pandemic, my restless web browsing introduced me to the world of international home exchange. Exploring further, I discovered a rich marketplace of possibilities. There were senior home exchanges, presumably with entrance ramps, grab bars in the bathrooms, and other essential amenities for old travelers, and LGBTQ exchanges, which I, as an L, found appealing. But there was little opportunity for me to be intersectional here. I had to prioritize one identity over the others. Well, I would wait and see what responses I got, hoping there would be seniors and middle-aged Ls among them.

Putting my home on the site required that I empty my surfaces of all but the most attractive of my tchotchkes; take inviting pictures; and write an effusive description of me, my home, the neighborhood, and the surrounding cultural and physical environment, using as many compelling adjectives as I could fit into the assigned boxes. Having practiced a decade earlier on dating sites, I was familiar with the function of mildly hyperbolic descriptions, posted my offering to the site, and waited for a deluge of enthusiastic exchangers.

Nothing. But during that prolonged time of nothing, I distracted myself by scrolling through all the charming or rustic or extravagant homes listed all over the world. I discovered that not all of these travelers wanted to come to America. Or if they did, they had children. Or pets. Having had both, I no longer wanted either in my home. Unless they were my own.

Eventually, after several requests for exchanges from the farthest exurbs of Perth, a ground-floor apartment in downtown Bangkok, and other dubious possibilities requiring a twenty-hour flight, there appeared an offering to exchange a four-bedroom stone farmhouse in the South of France for a month in July. I took a deep breath, wrote back with an enthusiastic yes, and set out to plan my practically free July in France. All that remained was to fill three bedrooms. I asked my closest unsuspecting and eventually delighted women friends to join me. Once they all agreed, the stage was set!

Months before my French adventure was to begin, I began to prepare by emptying, dusting, and replacing everything in my linen closet, concerned that my guests might examine the level of orderliness in my home. I didn't know anything about how home exchangers maintained their places, and I had my standards. While I didn't always live up to them, I still had them. Once my sheets and towels were more pristine than they had ever been, I scrubbed the drawer at the bottom of my stove, the place I keep my half-used aluminum foil and ruined cling wrap, which hadn't been thoroughly cleaned since I moved in. Clearly, I thought the cleanliness police (my fastidious long-dead mother in the guise of French home exchangers) were arriving, and I wanted to make a good impression.

Once I had coaxed all the fallen pushpins from the corners of closets and other unexpected locations, scrubbed all the doorknobs, and lined up my shoes in matching pairs, I moved to the task of learning to speak to other people while in France. French people.

I began to refresh my nearly dormant foreign-language skills by listening to French tapes that were guaranteed to teach even the most recalcitrant of pupils. Testimonials abounded. Dutifully, I began repeating the increasingly complex sentences and verb conjugations, developing my vocabulary and sense of the structure of the language. But what remained impenetrable was understanding French people speaking French.

Then, in the midst of my linguistic preparations, a friend introduced me to the website Wirecutter, a carefully curated resource for everything a traveler might ever need and everything they had no idea they ever would need—but really do. So onto the site I went.

Hand sanitizer. Wet wipes. Eye drops. Sleep masks. Noise-canceling headphones. Packing cubes. I was not an inexperienced traveler, and disinfecting wipes and eye drops were not high on my list when I was fifty. I just got on the plane, hoisted my bag into the overhead bin, and settled into my seat. Clearly a ten-hour flight at my age was going to require more amenities. Soon, Amazon packages began to arrive with increasing regularity. Compression stockings. Travel backpacks (important to keep hands free, they advise). Passport wallets. What if my bag got lost? Pack a change of clothes in my hands-free backpack. I hadn't yet even begun to read the travel books so I could anticipate where I was about to be going. I was still outfitting myself to be a responsible traveler.

Then things got complicated. The husband of one of

the women who was to join me became ill, and she was uncertain about whether he would be well enough for her to travel. Another received an ominous diagnosis and felt vulnerable about being so far from her doctor. *That's what happens when a bunch of old women try to make plans,* I told myself. *Real life interrupts everything. Be flexible,* I advised myself, advice I had been unsuccessfully giving myself all my life.

What could happen if none of them come and I'm alone in a stone farmhouse in a small village far from any city of significant size for an entire month? I thought. Now the reality of what I had set in motion became clear. I had committed to a month in a place where my language skills can be best described as eager American: too much smiling and not enough actual vocabulary. It's not that I don't enjoy my own company. I do. Quite a lot. I've happily lived alone for decades. But there is a Trader Joe's down the street. Most everyone speaks English—certainly better than I speak French. There are things I don't even think about but take entirely for granted. Movies. Blueberry yogurt. Library books.

Now I had a pickpocket-proof backpack with compartments for everything; waterproof hiking boots that only came in a neon color in my size (enormous, requiring men's shoes) so I looked as though I had two sparkling clubfeet and knew I would never ever under any circumstances wear them anywhere but in the privacy of France; travel insurance because, after all, I'm old and who knows what could happen to me; and a car rental in France because even with my hiking shoes, I would need a car. Now my budget for the next six months was shot. This had become the most expensive free vacation I'd ever had. But still . . . If everything worked out, if my friends could come, it would all be worth it.

My friends couldn't come.

While I felt apprehensive about being alone in a medieval village farmhouse and disappointed that I couldn't share the trip, I knew that if I created a reason not to go, even a good one, I'd be terribly disappointed in myself. And not wanting to have a future defined by disappointment, I went.

The compression stockings lasted less than an hour, my legs angrily rebelling against the experience of wearing a girdle, the eye drops rolled under my seat never to be retrieved, and I used one sanitizing cloth to wipe down the tray in front of me; the rest I inadvertently left behind in the seat pocket. My burglar-proof backpack was impossible to open without placing it on a flat surface before completely unzipping it, and consequently nearly unusable. My cross-body bag with all the sections (and little locks for each) was confusing since I never remembered which item was in which compartment, and I spent too much time opening and closing locks and zippers instead of doing what felt most natural: sticking my hand into a large pouch and rooting around for what I needed.

Arriving in Toulouse, I picked up the car and promptly set up its navigation system my phone's Google Maps, and the additionally rented GPS just in case the car and phone systems crashed, trusting that at least one would get me where I needed to go. I drove to the accompaniment of a cacophony of robotic voices all talking at once, flashing maps, and pointing arrows, resulting in an electronic confusion that led me to make four mistakes miscounting the number of exits from the endless number of roundabouts.

Two tense hours later, I arrived at the small twelfth-century village. Cars are not permitted on its narrow streets; they're kept in a designated field at the edge of town. I parked under a tree and gathered what I already knew was way too much stuff and set off, rolling and pulling my things across the rocky ground to the edge of the field where there was a metering machine placed prominently at the side of the paved road. After trying to remember the words for *day* and *week*, when it was my brief window of opportunity, I couldn't figure out where my credit card went or how much time my choices allowed me, and feeling the impatient shifting of people behind me, I abandoned my place, silently promising to return to the parking meter's linguistic and electronic mysteries later, and wobbled forward.

Crossing the wide boulevard in the center of town, feeling light-headed from the global record-breaking heat wave descending upon Europe, I lurched toward an outdoor café, precipitously lowered myself onto an entirely too-small wrought-iron chair, and in my best French asked for directions to 8 rue Magéne. No one appeared to know, but just before the ignominious longing for someone—anyone—to spring forth from somewhere—anywhere—and take care of me arose, the dishwasher who was standing nearby overheard my halting question and mercifully knew that the rue was merely two rues away. He pointed me in the right direction, and I set off, embarrassed that my entry into France was, so far, decidedly inauspicious.

After hundreds of hours of dutifully repeating words, tenses, and conjugations, my French had improved from word by halting word to sentence by labored sentence. I wasn't up to paragraph by graceful paragraph yet. Not by a long shot. I was still worried about being able to follow the speed of native French speakers but was reassured that the woman who was to welcome me and show me around the house was a British expat. But she had, what was to my American ears, an extremely thick accent and spoke in quick bursts, leaving most of her explanations almost entirely unintelligible, and I was too hot, too tired, and too desperately in need of a shower to do more than amiably nod, my fallback demeanor when at a loss for what to do. She left me with a tangle of keys, a fresh baguette, some wilted lettuce, and presumably a full description of everything I needed to know about the house. After I deposited my luggage and splashed cold water on my face, my maiden voyage at navigating the small village market while attempting to communicate in my limited French resulted in a dinner consisting of boxed gazpacho and olives, followed by a bowl of Special K and bananas.

The farmhouse was stone, all the shutters were shuttered, and the interior was relievedly cool and dark. The banister-free stairs wound up to a second floor, requiring that every single ascent and descent be precise, with first my left, then my right foot placed firmly upon each step before continuing onward. There was a voluble Siamese cat that came with the home exchange (I am most decidedly not a cat person). My welcomer neglected to mention—at least I think she did—that the church bells rang every hour on the hour. All night. Also, that when the bells chimed, the cat either cried or sang; it was unclear which, since I am entirely unable to interpret the intention of cat sounds.

When, as a much younger woman, I had first traveled to France, I approached the counterman in the coffee shop near my hotel and proudly intoned, "Un cappuccino, s'il vous plaît." There was a long pause, which he pointedly filled by saying, "Bonjour, madame."

Oops, I thought. *The French begin with hello. I am rude and have just become an ugly American. Always begin with bonjour.* That lesson firmly in place, I have always been careful to begin with a warm hello whenever I go into a shop or speak to a salesperson.

I entered the local patisserie the next morning, nervously rehearsing all the words I would need to purchase a baguette, milk, a vegetable quiche, and a lemon tart. Remembering my good manners, but forgetting the right word, I enthusiastically bellowed *"Aujourd'hui!"* to the startled shopkeeper. I kept talking even after recognizing my mistake, given that she was the gatekeeper to the food I intended to eat that day, but painstakingly bonjoured my way through the rest of my stay.

Later that morning, there was a sturdy knock on the front door. I opened it to the eager faces of friends of my hosts who had been asked to look in on me to see if I needed anything, which I took to mean that seeing as I am startlingly old to be traveling alone, they should see if I needed their help.

The English-speaking husband had mansplaining down to a fine art, even writing out for me tasks that I had already managed to figure out on my own. He spoke, and his wife smiled at him until he apparently said something entirely incorrect, at which point she gently remonstrated and rephrased his mistake. I reminded myself that running a home, even a French home where many of the details are different, was something I had been doing for nearly sixty years. Not rocket science. I was not sure what a hob was—something about the stove, I thought—but I'd figure it out.

I had carefully learned the French words for an extensive range of foods, predicated on the assumption that I would be talking to shopkeepers and asking for aubergines or chèvre. But unless I drove nearly an hour to a supermarché, which felt both too generic and linguistically daunting, I ate what the village market had in stock that day, filling my sack with unfamiliar cheeses, random olives, tomatoes, more gazpacho (I could read those labels), a wide range of chocolate, and take-out tabbouleh. I added peaches and nectarines but soon discovered that they ripened, turning mushy and brown within hours in the relentless heat, so I resorted to adding three melons daily, one for each meal. My imaginings of daily outings to cafés where I would feast on duck breast and crème brûlée evaporated as the heat rose to nearly unbreathable heights.

Each morning, I awakened at six, before the sun was high in the sky. I filled my thermos with iced coffee, put my phone in my pocket (although I had no one to call if there had been an actual emergency), and set out through the sleeping streets, carefully placing my sneakered American feet on the uneven cobblestones, moving alongside the graceful abbey to a path winding down to the river that ran behind the village.

By the end of the first week, I had defined the contours of my constitutional into the vineyards on a well-marked path past some working farms, leading up an incline to a paved road that circled around the back of the village and returned me to the abbey, across another narrow bridge and onto a paved path to the patisserie where I purchased my morning *pain aux raisins*. After saying bonjour. This began the day, and a rum raisin ice cream cone at the riverside café concluded it.

At the end of the second week, I came upon the Saturday market in the local square, filled with food stalls, artists' displays, and colorful women's clothing hanging from tall poles. Buzzing around all the offerings were French women, all appearing to be cool, all charmingly dressed, speaking with rapidity to one another and the vendors. Hastily wiping away the rivulets of sweat making their way down my face and falling off my chin, I feigned interest in the displays, feeling ungainly, like Gulliver on his travels. Having been six feet tall once upon a much younger time, I was still many inches above everyone there, and as the reminders of a gangling adolescence surfaced, I arranged my face in what I hoped was a benign expression and walked briskly past all the booths as if I had somewhere important to be. Stopping in the patisserie for something comforting, something that would briefly allow me to feel like an ordinary-size person, I stood in a long line for my morning pastry as people chatted too fast for me to understand anything but their remarkable inability to feel the heat.

Later that afternoon, I walked down to the river where families were delightedly splashing in the blessedly cool water. My intention was to glide to its edge, effortlessly unfold myself onto the ground, and read, imagining myself in a painting by somebody who painted old women lounging along the banks of a river. But as I grew closer, I realized that the water was gently lapping against rocks, with only an intermittent boulder upon which there was no way I could gracefully unfold. I sat down on a piece of stone that hit my behind in an untoward way and tried to look comfortable, eventually sliding closer to the ground until I was, as I had originally intended, sitting on the shore. The rocky shore. After an appropriate interval during which, if anyone were watching, I might have been reading, I carefully moved to all fours and pushed down, which is how I get up off the ground now. I straightened up and didn't look around to see if anyone had witnessed my unceremonious rise and, for the rest of my stay, enjoyed the river from afar.

I intermittently considered trying to be productive, returning home with the rough draft of a manuscript resting smugly in my computer. Or finally getting to all the first-generation immigrant experience novels I had been meaning to read. Or learning how to make photo albums from the thousands of pictures scattered throughout my computer, arranging them gracefully, then adding music, resulting in a lovely show-and-tell upon my return that would impress my old friends, none of whom have nearly that level of technological skill. I could read about the Cathar history of the region, one apparently obliterated by the Catholic version, or visit the abbey and educate myself about their history of this landscape. All of that was possible, but I didn't want to do any of it.

I have had what I called my "bathrobe" days at home, when I did nothing but eat popcorn, read a novel, watch some television, look out the window, and maybe after many hours complete a minimal task like a load of laundry or running the dishwasher. But I never had two days in a row of "bathrobe." Now I have weeks.

Before I embarked on this solitary adventure, I sensed I would return home knowing things about myself that I didn't know when I left. And I did. I was surprised by the ease with which I sank into the rhythms and beauty of the natural world and small village life— two realities about which I know very little. I can't tell the difference between a chestnut and a maple tree. And villages are places my grandparents fled.

Another set of possibilities opened to me. Ones where I didn't need or want anything more than what was before me, the quiet a balm and a comfort. Perhaps I no longer needed to protect myself against a childhood where the silence that saturated our home bristled with angry and dangerous possibility. Perhaps I didn't have to fill every pause in conversation with carefully chosen words. Or be the woman I so needed then. Perhaps I no longer had to be smart or interesting, engaged or responsive, or to ask the most penetrating question or always consider how to be helpful. Perhaps, at eighty-three, I am, just a little bit, free.

AND THEN THERE WAS THE PANDEMIC

ONE

I live alone, and if I get COVID, I won't have any help unless I become hospitalized. Those are the scary facts. Nevertheless, I am personally not in an emergency. The world is; poor and vulnerable people are; emergency workers, struggling families, immigrants, homeless people, first responders are. They are in an emergency. But I am, most certainly, in something.

When stringent quarantine rules are mandated, I spend hours thoroughly cleaning, scrubbing small spots out of my carpeting and vacuuming the corners of my closets. Creating and maintaining scrupulous cleanliness allows me a fleeting sense of authority over my environment. At least the immediate one.

TWO

I walk early every morning when the path along the water's edge is still empty, except for the most determined bikers or runners. I keep my mask down around my neck and pull it up when I see a human approaching. Upon arriving home, I scrub the mask, my hands, and my face in case something landed on my few centimeters of exposed skin. By then it is 9:00 a.m., and I am safely tucked in for the day. Danger-free until tomorrow morning. No Cossacks on horseback requiring me to flee to a root cellar. Just an invisible particle in the air.

THREE

Today is the eighteenth anniversary of my mother's death. I light a candle, prop up a picture of the two of us dancing at my eldest daughter's first wedding, and feel her presence as I move through the day.

Like me, my mother was a mediocre cook. In addition to a dry and crumbly date-and-nut loaf, her alternative festive dessert was a Jell-O mold with little pieces of fruit quivering in its lime recesses. My environment is calm, beautiful, and cushioning like a protective aspic. I'm the trapped grape.

FOUR

It's my eighty-second birthday. I plan to delight in the fragrance of flowers sent by my friends and daughters. Choose one of the novels awaiting me. Fill my living room with exuberant music. I even put on cute clothes for the first time since all the lockdowns began. And earrings. I will write and watch TV, but no news. Not today. Today will be for pleasure only. Let's see if I can do it.

Noon: so far, so good. As I prepare to settle in with the pint of caramel-swirl ice cream for lunch—no need for a bowl—my oldest friend, masked and gloved, appears at my door holding a lemon poppy seed cake with cream cheese frosting. My favorite. I cover my face as I stand in the doorway, the closest I've been to anyone in weeks, and fight the urge to throw my arms around her. I thank her, and she says something to me that I can't hear from behind her mask, but I assume they are the loving birthday-wishes kind of words.

For the first time in my life, I am alone as I light the candles, make my wish, and blow them out. I don't have to cut the first piece, pass slices around while talking to all my guests. Instead, I eat the cake like a child, dispensing with the fork entirely and delighting in sucking the frosting off my fingers. Utensils take so much of the pleasure out of eating. I have lived my whole life without ever noticing that.

FIVE

Reports of the pandemic's spread have become more ominous, and the projections of how long we might have to quarantine have lengthened. Straightening my arthritic shoulders, I decide to do what my mother called "taking myself in hand." I take myself in both hand and foot and prepare to give myself a pedicure, both affirming and decorating my body.

I have pedicures during the summer months because my toes stick out of my sandals and I feel attractive when they're painted. Although no one sees them but me, I continue to embellish them in an ever-changing range of colors all year. Through more critical and evaluative eyes, it's a preposterous indulgence, but when I take off my crew socks at night or look down in the shower and see them lustrous in subtle shades of mauve or taupe, I feel quite lovely. From the ankles down anyway.

The first problem of this self-directed pedicure presents itself at once. I don't actually know how to paint my own toes. I can't bend my knees enough to see what's going on with them. I polish my glasses, hoping they will somehow serve to magnify them, realize they won't, go to my drawer, and retrieve my actual magnifying glass and inspect my toes. Not good. Not good at all.

They're entirely overgrown, kind of like my hair, but

I won't even entertain the thought of doing anything to my hair. That requires skill. Toenails just require cutting and maybe pushing the cuticles around a bit. I can do that. In fact, I'll put some red polish on my toes just to brighten up the landscape a little bit. And while I'm at it, I'll push the cuticles on my fingernails around as well.

I begin the process with foot cream to soften up my unattended skin using an Israeli product from across the Green Line in the occupied territories, also known as Palestine. It was a gift from someone who didn't know better. I haven't wanted to use it and feel guilty about even having it, but not guilty enough to throw it away. After all, the sin of purchasing it has already been committed. My self-protective analysis in place, I smooth the politically corrupt cream into my feet and rub it in. *Why have I waited so long to do this?* I wonder. *It feels splendid.* I massage until my feet are like a baby's behind. Well, not really, but certainly softer than they have been in a long time.

Becoming more focused, I put vitamin E oil on my toes and start pushing my cuticles from here to there, not able to see what I'm doing, just making little circles and hoping the cuticles are getting the message.

Now for the cutting. I start small, with my little toe, and painstakingly position the nail clippers over the toenail and press. Bingo! Somewhere on my carpet resides my toenail. Since I don't want my bedroom carpet littered with parts of my body, I place a towel under my feet, something I probably should have done from the start. With growing certainty, I clip my nails, and only once do I draw blood. Not a lot, but clearly the result of a poor positioning of the clipper. Or undeserved overconfidence.

Then it's time for the emery board, except I can't see where to emery. I turn to the magnifying glass to inspect the shape of my clips to see what needs to be filed down, try to memorize what I see, put down the glass, and begin.

I emery my nails by feel, and if my fingers don't bump into any sharp or rough edges, I figure I've done a good-enough job. I'm ready to paint my toenails a bright celebratory red.

I stuff clumps of Kleenex between my toes, place both feet on the towel littered with errant nails, shake the bottle like I know what I'm doing, and begin with the little toe. That's the one with the smallest nail, so of course I get polish on the toe and much of the neighboring vicinity. But I remain optimistic and decide I'll get a Q-tip with nail polish remover when I'm done and erase all my boundary-crossing errors ther..

By the time I move to the second foot, I seem to have gotten the hang of it and get most of the polish on the actual toenail and a bit less on the toe. Finishing, I lean back and gaze down at what looks like two very large, partially melted red popsicles.

As the paint hardens and dries, I tell myself that this was a first attempt and I'll get better at it over time, which leads me to dispiriting thoughts about all the quarantined time ahead. I click on my screen and discover that Ben Affleck is out of rehab and has a new girlfriend. Time passes.

SIX

During these endless months, I've watched hours of YouTube cooking demonstrations and have learned how to candy orange peels and frost and decorate a cake that I've presumably just made, but never will. I study pictures of the middle-aged Olsen twins with carefully curated girls' faces, who marry and divorce wealthy and powerful men. It's not clear what else they do. I read magazines that alert the reader to the coupling and decoupling of thirtysomething movie stars I've never heard of. All this drifting puts me in a kind of trance where I am not here. Not in this moment. Not even in my body, except for the desire for fried clams and pistachio ice cream, my two favorites when I was a girl sitting in a booth at Howard Johnson's while imagining a grown-up future that most decidedly did not include an old woman wearing neither sneakers nor bra, padding around her condo, spending another day in quarantine.

THE KITCHEN IS CLOSED

I don't cook anymore. Nothing that requires sautéing onions and garlic, laboriously peeling or chopping large piles of vegetables, or even creating a marinade and dunking dinner in it for a couple of hours. I do watch Ina Garten, who effortlessly and with great delight prepares glorious meals. I sometimes imagine that I'm Sandy/Ina, setting long farm tables overflowing with a cornucopia of sweet and savory food, all artfully displayed, wild and fresh flowers from the garden that I've never had, and whatever other requisite accompaniments to the meal I will never make.

But I do have my dishes. Four to be exact. Over the years, whenever I have been pressed to bring a dish for a potluck, I cycle one of the four into service, counting on the fact that I won't have brought the same dish to the same group over the past several years and they will have forgotten the last time I did and not get wise to my limited repertoire.

Pomegranate chicken is a great favorite. My chicken salad rocks. Caprese salad probably doesn't really qualify as a dish, mostly requiring slicing and chiffonading basil. I love meatloaf, which I make with a pork, beef, and lamb combo, but nobody eats meatloaf anymore, so it's rarely pressed into service.

When my kids were little—forever ago—I made franks and beans with maple syrup and a latticework of bacon strips on the top. My specialties have improved since that prosaic beginning, but I never smile when I'm cooking like Ina does. I have a friend who tells me she finds cooking meditative. I don't even find meditation meditative.

I always feel that the time I'm spending making a meal that will be eaten in twenty minutes and leave a dirty kitchen could be better spent reading a book, and sometimes, often catastrophically, I try to combine cooking and reading, resulting in either a burned dish or a final product missing an ingredient, a seasoning, or the necessary stirring that might have kept it from congealing.

When I was a young wife in the 1950s, my dinner repertoire consisted of what constituted fancy cooking for white suburban housewives: beef stroganoff, chicken divan, and Swedish meatballs. At my first dinner party I served a half grapefruit with a maraschino cherry propped cheerfully at its center for the first course. I hadn't yet learned that there was an urgent need to separate the grapefruit sections first, and my guests were left to politely prod, then more assertively jab as best they could as grapefruit juice squirted everywhere.

My divorce released me from many things, among them the need to make food for entertaining. I just made food for eating. And as simply as I could. After I returned from work carrying groceries and herding two little girls into our apartment at 5:45, dinner needed to be quick. And it was. I leaned toward the nutritious but could be easily swayed depending on how stressful the day had been. Celebrations, perhaps of a good grade, a part in the school play (not as a tree or any inanimate object though; they had to have speaking lines to qualify), or a well-received report on a school trip, were marked by my use of the melon scooper, which allowed little balls of cantaloupe to rest atop a larger scoop of orange sherbet. The fruit provided symmetry and a nutritional balance to the sweet. Sometimes when we ran out of money, I made dinner with food coloring so the mashed potatoes, rice, or spaghetti, bought with what was left at the end of the month, looked redly or greenly festive.

Then there was the grim healthy period of brown rice and vegetables, carrot juice and make-believe meat for make-believe hamburgers—my body a temple. I had an enormous rice cooker, a steamer for the incessant vegetables, and a juicer for the organic carrots, sometimes augmented with parsley and beets. After several years of this relentless discipline, I had a vivid dream. I was on U Street in Washington, DC, standing outside the best ribs restaurant in the neighborhood. I could smell them cooking, imagine the greasy drip of my first bite and the thick, gloriously sated feeling of eating too much meat. I concluded upon awakening that my body wanted meat, as if it were speaking directly to me. Meat led me down the slippery slope of carbs, sweets, and all the other delicious, no-longer-forbidden foods.

But during all those culinary eras, I never actually learned how to cook. In my forties, I entered a long-term partnership in which it was incumbent upon me to prepare dinners. She was an adult who couldn't be distracted with cartoons and Cheerios or a grilled cheese with bacon. I had to prepare real food. And I did, but even then, the most unsatisfying parts of my day were thinking about what we would eat, getting it, preparing it, cooking it. Everything took time away from things I wanted to be thinking about and places I wanted to be instead of the kitchen. She, on the other hand, loved to cook—exotic, elaborate dinners involving shallot, ginger, tamarind, and other flavors I had only encountered in restaurants. I had to up my game. We alternated dinners, so I had to produce three and sometimes four splendid dinners every week that would do justice to her culinary efforts and let her know I took them and her seriously.

I took to watching *The Galloping Gourmet*, and Graham Kerr became my guide to kitchen fluency. I poached. I blended. I ground. I chopped, macerated, grated, and whisked and turned out some pretty good meals. But it always felt like an awful lot of work for the aforementioned twenty minutes of yummy eating and being left with a decimated kitchen.

Don't get me wrong. I can turn out a Thanksgiving dinner. It's not great, but it's friendly, and with enough wine, people don't notice that the turkey is a bit dry, the gravy hasn't really thickened, the brussels sprouts smell funny, and the cranberry sauce comes from a can. But the conversation flows as does the wine, and with several store-bought pies, all ends well. But the entire enterprise takes days, endless lists, and at least one of my fingers decorated with a bandage.

Mercifully now, my condo has a very small, narrow galley kitchen. The merciful part is that such a bare-bones kitchen (with particleboard cabinets and whimsical knobs that I added to make everything look a bit less drab) doesn't demand culinary excellence. It's a functional space in which to prepare functional meals. Which I do.

Still, when I'm called upon to participate in a group meal, I'm always the assigned sous-chef and, at its conclusion, the one who fills the dishwasher. I'm good at both those tasks. The oohing and aahing go to other women, and that's OK with me.

I have cycled through envy, shame, and embarrassment over the decades, but now, at this late stage of my life, I have arrived at the pinnacle of spiritual and psychological health: I can defrost, and I can order in. That works for me.

CONFESSIONS OF AN AUTODIDACT

The pinnacle of my excellence as a student began and ended in fourth grade. Proudly raising my hand, getting called on, having the right answer, then receiving a smiling acknowledgment from Mrs. Lamb, who told me I was a smart little girl, were things that I could only count on that year. I limped forward in my academic life from that high point, the gulf between schoolwork and what I wanted and needed to know for my real life widening with each passing year.

From the time I was able to go to the library on my own, I read indiscriminately until I discovered an author I loved, then took out all their other books. I was too shy to ask the librarian for help, although I don't know what I would have asked even if I had been able to. It was the books themselves that were transporting, the sense of entering an imaginary landscape where people came to life, where I could hear their voices when they spoke, feel their feelings, and share in their triumphs. In the 1940s everything I read ended in some kind of triumph.

Eventually books became not only a portal to how other people lived, but a resource that might help me figure out who I wanted to become. In the early 1950s, white men wrote to explain the world and what it felt like to be them. Their novels felt operatic to me, evoking lives of adventure, first losing, then finding themselves, every character so much more intense than anyone in my teenage life. I fell in love with Sydney Carton and recognized parts of myself in Holden Caulfield. But Marjorie Morningstar was my first exposure to a girl who found her way out of and well beyond the constraints that were intended to define her. Of course, it ended badly, but I planned to figure out a way to avoid her suburban fate, the one I would leave in my not yet clear but dramatic wake. I wanted to "open up a mouth" as my grandmother would have said, but I also wanted to be a successful performer like Marjorie, standing in a spotlight before a rapt audience. I hadn't yet figured out whether I would sing, dance, or act to generate the attention I dreamed of. I also intended to be very smart in something, although it wasn't clear to me just what.

My scholarship throughout high school was decidedly average, after which I entered a midwestern university. That first exposure to college life lasted for less than one semester, at the end of which the dean of women sternly informed my mortified parents that I wasn't ready to prepare for my adult life. I was, in her words, "consorting with undesirable elements," code for local Black people, who, like me, loved jazz and with whom I spent many hours listening to and passionately discussing the music and the pros and cons of the emerging style of bebop.

She was right about one thing. I wasn't ready. I didn't return to college for decades, after substituting my fledgling attempt at a formal education for a too-early marriage, the inevitable divorce that followed, the exhausting demands of single motherhood, and my enthusiastic immersion in the political and cultural shifts that marked the convulsive American decade of the 1960s.

I returned to college in my midthirties and enrolled in a degree program created for working adult students with families, guided by a cultivated and witty New York woman who encouraged me forward inch by painstaking inch. Our correspondence was punctuated by suggestions of books or articles I might enjoy, with invitations to let her know what I thought about them. My reading slowly deepened as did her questions and challenges, and after three years, my final thesis became a book, a feminist critique of child sexual abuse.

After its publication, I was received by an eager audience of women who were appreciative that I had named and opened a public conversation about such a ubiquitous but unacknowledged reality. I became a woman who neither sang, danced, nor acted. Instead, I organized survivors, taught therapists and social workers, and gave fierce speeches studded with calls to action. Although I had never formally studied philosophy, sociology, political theory, economics, or anything that would have been required in a conventional college, I was now viewed as a well-educated woman with a master's degree, whose thinking, analysis, and proposal for advocacy was eagerly sought by a growing number of mental health professionals and scholars.

Yet whenever I was on a panel where statistical tables were introduced, intended to explain deviation and probability, I always worried I'd be asked to respond to a visual that resembled nothing more than a multicolored, random geometric line drawing with occasional, seemingly arbitrary curves. If I attended a talk about feminism within a Foucauldian framework, and in those days, there were many, I was determined to try just once more to understand him. But I never did. Either try or understand. My feminist analysis was repeatedly challenged by dense psychoanalytic interpretations of male behaviors where issues of addiction, communication, and impulse control were defined as the etiology of child abuse (which inevitably identified their mothers or wives as the genesis of male sexual "acting out"). In my responses, I leaped forcefully into passionate moral and ethical outrage that I felt deeply, but also served to mask all the crevices of my ignorance. I had never gotten to those books. And probably wouldn't. I had learned how to think but still couldn't follow anything beyond elementary statistics, basic philosophy, and midlevel psychoanalysis. Nor could I write a correct footnote or a formal essay, or place semicolons correctly.

Thankfully, my stately body lent unearned gravitas to my words. I had become an imposing middle-aged woman who had access to a wide-ranging and compelling vocabulary after a lifetime of reading. People took me seriously. My words mattered. Sometimes when I was speaking to a large audience, I imagined myself with my hands on my hips, "opening up a big mouth." I did better than Marjorie Morningstar ever did. No suburbs for me. I delivered jeremiads, not speeches. Diatribes, not challenges. I had become a proudly self-educated woman. Mostly.

In an animated argument about the dangerous political repercussions of Facebook, the assumption appeared to be that everyone already knew how algorithms work. I didn't and never have. But a well-placed nod accompanied by an agreeable *hmm* allowed my ignorance to remain invisible. In a discussion of a current book that might reference Minerva or someone goddess- or godlike rising from the sea or falling from the sky, I remained silent. I knew who the Greek gods were and what each represented in eighth grade, but only Jason and the golden fleece came to settle permanently in my memory. All the rest made their brief appearance, then fled. I deflected with a question.

I've crashed upon the shoals of plots of books written by women I admire who have taken a myth and made it their central metaphor. I look up the myth but am sure that I miss all the subtleties. Also, the sky itself is both literally and figuratively beyond me, as are the names and locations of constellations, the planets, and their relationships to one another and the sun. Furthermore, everything having to do with meteorology is a complete blank. Whenever there is a climate emergency, the television announcers show rapidly spinning colored circles presumably revealing patterns of hurricanes or tornadoes punctuated by cold and warm fronts that move in seemingly random directions. But when I'm in conversation about the weather—which, living in California, is more often than you might imagine— murmuring something dire about climate change allows me to skirt a potential analysis of both kinds of fronts and why they move at the rate of speed they do with a graceful sidestep.

When I'm making my way through a dense political or literary article and have to return and reread something because I can't understand it, I don't assume the author was either a poor writer, a garbled thinker, or simply not making sense. It's me. My failings. My inadequacies. And don't even get me started about Emily Dickinson. She became the central metaphor of my shame. I've always intended to take a class on Emily Dickinson because I felt so inadequate to make my way into her language, but I never have. And that's the heart of it. Shame has never been enough for me to alter my behavior. I simply tuck it alongside the delights of reading what I love, learning more about what matters to me. They have been twinned, one unable to alter the other all my life.

But it's not just what I don't know. It's what I imagined everyone else did: people with a formal, a proper, a consecutive education who have been exposed to all those subjects, with at least a glancing relationship with broad, general bodies of knowledge. My personal bodies are already deep and ever deepening, but they don't surface in social situations as often as I hoped they would. The Art Ensemble of Chicago and its relationship to the early compositions of Thelonious Monk or Bud Powell just don't emerge over dinner. Or over anything for that matter. On the other hand, neither does Emily Dickinson.

But now I'm an old woman, and much of what inhibited my life has eroded. Protecting myself against how I may be seen or judged feels like a doomed and exhausting enterprise, and I've decided to trust that Mrs. Lamb had been right. I was a smart girl.

I no longer track the fiction and nonfiction best-seller and international awards lists. They fueled my insecurity, serving as substitutes for someone, anyone, to provide me with a list of books to read, at the conclusion of which I would be educated. And smart. College-educated smart.

I read only what I want to and have released myself from the self-criticism of never having fully understood the revered authors I assume well-educated people have, nor do I feel the demands of the current wunder-kinder of the literary lists. I gravitate to what has always drawn me. Sweeping, well-populated stories filled with complicated people. No minimalism for me. I am still that same young girl who wanted books to teach her how people inhabited their lives, contemplated their dreams and their losses, and found their way to something that approximated meaning. Whenever I open a new volume, the exhilaration of feeling poised at the portal of a new world has never left me.

I rarely try to appear smart anymore. I'm smart enough. I don't have to be anything at all, the external markers of my hard-won education no longer necessary. My bookshelves have been thinned to only my most be-loved books, the ones to which I return again and again. The ones that help me remember how complicated it is to be a human being. How language can sing. And how, as my Jewish grandfather told me, "They can take everything from you except what's in your mind. So fill it up with magical things." And I have.

KEEPING UP

Either everything is getting faster, or I've slowed down to a crawl. I've decided to go with the former. It seems that it was just Wednesday four days ago, yet it's Wednesday again now and there are three novels, two essay collections, a Danish mystery, a book of poetry, and a growing pile of *New Yorker*s awaiting me. With more on their way.

And there are, as there has always been, a half dozen critical reviews and more general cultural assessments accompanying each book. Was the intention of the author achieved? In what ways? And how does this book fit into this cultural moment? What questions does it illuminate and how? When time once permitted, I completed the book, formed my opinions, then compared my views with thinkers I respected. But it seems that time is coming so fast now that I find myself careening between an article about an idea from two books back and something new about an entirely different subject. I simply can't keep up.

I have distinct categories where I'm well read, where I understand the roots, trunk, and branches of the subject matter. But new leaves keep blossoming. Just as soon as I feel current, a new analysis, critique, novelistic interpretation, or book of poetry addressing the subject matter at hand is published. Is it that more leaves are being published or that I'm reading more slowly?

Then there's the news, which also seems to be at a different tempo than it once was. I still feel a gleeful pride when I score at least eight out of eleven on the *New York Times* weekly news quiz. That inconsequential success fills me with the temporary confidence that I'm keeping up. The news—called in high school "current events"—continues to matter to me. I work at it, checking the headlines on my iPad first thing in the morning, reading several newspapers, following online sites, and watching TV news in the evening. I'm entirely current. With America anyhow. The complexities of Iran and Iraq, the Saudi proxy wars, and Somalia elude me, much as I put my mind to learning about them, even reading long articles in the *New Yorker* written to explain such global intricacies to their educated readership. I glaze over, skim, try to read the last paragraph in the hope it will condense everything that came before, and I will have a successful takeaway. But it doesn't, and I don't.

My news consumption is augmented with essays by journalists I admire, feminists from my generation who are still passionately opining, as well as the current activists on Twitter, many women of color who are engaged in rich conversation with one another when they are not writing urgent essays and necessarily discomforting books. *We are in good hands,* I always think as read them. Which leaves me feeling current and very much in the know. Or at least, in those specific knows.

Once, my study was lined with bookcases containing my prized collection of feminists' first novels. I delighted in reading everything that followed from each woman's literary beginnings. What stories were they going to tell during a period of such dramatic societal change? I followed their careers as closely as I had the dating life of Ava Gardner during my teenage years.

Over the decades my cultural life expanded to include movies, theater, and dance, but increasingly, they have fallen away. The traffic is too bad, the sound is too low, the price is too high, the crowds are unruly, and the subject matter rarely seems to include well-drawn old women. I should make more of an effort, I suppose, but it's the effort part that slows me down. Without my noticing, there was a cutoff moment, or series of moments, when keeping up began to recede in both importance and pleasure.

Then there is my hearing. Both my lack of it and the current speed of words leave me in the dust. They come at me faster than they used to. Consider the tempo of Carmen McRae and that of Beyoncé. While I am a proud member of the Beyhive and admire her both musically and politically, words fly out of her mouth, blur, and evaporate, and she's on to the next phrase before I can figure out what she's just said. I trust it's something I'd agree with and would applaud but am not sure exactly what it is. Closed captions would help, but music videos don't have them.

I had the same experience with *Hamilton*. The lyrics raced past, creating waves of exuberant sound, but the actual content would have required my following the lyrics in a printed program. At least the blues repeat each line twice so if you miss it the first time, you get a second chance. Contemporary culture is exuberantly passing me by.

And as it recedes into the near distance, I'm more able to give myself permission to read only what I really want to. A big, sprawling story with lots of characters, lots of complexities, lots of feelings, and lots of intensity.

Now, when I review lists of potential novels or movies vying for my attention and purchase, my resistance centers on the subject matter. Those that are not centered on an unreliable narrator (currently very much in vogue), are about young people coming of age, the struggle to balance one's work and personal life, daughters coming to terms with complicated mothers (my sympathies are always with the mother), and every conceivable form of middle-aged angst no longer hold my full attention for the required minimum of 250 pages. Novels about immigration, emigration, exile, and the complexities of multiple identities engage me as long as the character isn't twenty or thirty. Or even forty. Most of all, I long for stories about aging and already-aged people. Women in particular.

I cringe to think that I've become an old woman set in her ways, but it's true. I have. I do my best not to let that be publicly known though. I'm careful not to start my sentences with "back in the day," unless, of course, I'm in conversation with a woman with whom I shared that long-ago day. I don't dismiss contemporary artists as inevitably a derivative of the beloved originator who made it all possible (although I often do have that thought), and force myself to remember that lineages are, by their very definition, in motion. Those that came before opened the possibilities for those who follow. But still.

I read. That's always been at the heart of my way. Ketchup bottles, cereal boxes, prescription instructions: my young eyes were always searching for print upon which to settle. Whenever I needed to understand a complicated moment in my life, I read books to show me how other people—women mostly, but not always—dealt with the realities of identity or faith, death or change. Where they found clarity and courage. How they managed to keep going, if that was the best they could do in the moment. And the books I wrote were those that hadn't yet been written for the woman I once was, who would be looking for them.

Even though I took both pride and pleasure in all the ways I was conversant with the latest novels, albums (they were albums then), and movies that were all right on the tip of my proud tongue, now what I want is to sink into the language of other old ladies. Or at least middle-aged writers creating old women characters. Or their old mothers. Complex old mothers only. No more singularly bad ones. I want more Olive Kitteridge. Margaret Atwood's women. Sigrid Nunez's friendships. I want to read stories about what it feels like to grow old. To lose family and friends. To struggle with faith and spirit. To prepare to die. I read now to find my own life echoed on the page. To feel less alone.

I imagine taking a walk with Olive and talking about everything, insofar as Olive would even talk to me. We would stride along covering great distances together as the day began, wearing sensible shoes and being comfortable with long silences. When we spoke, it would be about how we are drawing close to the end of things. I want to be in the company of women who write about what it feels like to draw close. I am firmly set in that way.

There is more life behind me than ahead, and I want my reading to be a time to reflect and to come to terms with what it has all been. I want to be in the company of women who write about that. I want to keep up with them. I can't keep up with all the rest of it. The world will hurtle forward with me relievedly waving in the rearview mirror.

AN EPITAPH FOR
MY MEMORY

My memory has gone the way of my upper arms. It's softened and it wobbles. My proper nouns have been evaporating for over a decade, and I've learned to keep going when a specific name, place, or object has absconded, instead of pausing and looking confused. Now, to add insult to injury, when I'm telling a proper-noun-less story and a splendid illuminating detail certain to enhance my enthusiastic narration surfaces, I no longer reach for it because I've had to painfully acknowledge that I won't be able to find my way back to wherever it was I was trying to go.

Replacing the evaporated nouns and details are irrelevant pieces of information that have taken root like weeds alongside the highway. At the market, I'm less able now to keep track of whether I'm either low or out of a staple that is critical to the functioning of my kitchen, so just to be on the safe side, I'll buy another. As of this writing, I have four jars of Hellmann's mayo, two Heinz ketchups, two mango chutneys, and three bags of low-salt almonds taking up precious space on my kitchen shelves. Not that I don't have a well-ordered shopping list. I do. It remains poised, ready for service on my desk long after I drive away from the house.

And as I forget what I want to say or buy or do, I remember what doesn't and never did matter. My mind is cluttered with obscure facts about Xavier Cugat, who was born on January 1, 1900, and Louis Armstrong, who claimed to be, and copious details about the early lives of Rock Hudson, Tab Hunter, and Farley Granger, whose posters filled my bedroom walls (before I knew they were all gay and consequently unavailable to appreciate my teenaged longing). I've retained the names and histories of all of Elizabeth Taylor's husbands—in order (Richard Burton twice)—as well as the disheartening details of the early childhoods and marital adventures of Ava Gardner, Judy Garland, and Billie Holiday. The lyrics to Jerome Kern's ballads are on the tip of my tongue, but what I need at the pharmacy evaporates between my house and the store. My eye drops are more critical than the words to "Smoke Gets in Your Eyes," but my memory does not give them that priority.

All this accumulated detritus is taking up precious

brain space I need for new information that matters in the here and now. Like, how can I program my exercise on my Apple Watch when everything is so much smaller than my fingertips? (Answer: a chopstick.) And how do I create a semblance of order with all those photographs on my computer? (No answer yet.)

I read scholarly articles about the relationship between aging and memory but am unable to understand the complexities of synaptic plasticity. The synapses between my brain cells are dropping. My neurons are shrinking, my dendrites retracting, and the fatty myelin that wraps around my axons is deteriorating. I have no idea what or where my dendrites are and why my axons are losing their myelin. But their decline appears to be an anatomical inevitability.

Given that I live in a capitalist economy, there is of course a niche created to address these slippages. It's "memory fitness," a lucrative focus for entrepreneurs who invite my mind to engage in "fun workouts," daily calisthenics so I and it remain agile. Think of it as a facelift for the brain. There are games, tricks, mnemonic devices, uses of either technology or yellow Post-it notes, depending on individual proficiencies. Initially I scorned the idea but now admit to feeling relief and a rush of pride when I pass a test or win a game, even as I dismiss those I fail as foolish and not indicative of anything. I continue to dedicate myself to these cognitive exercises and augment my already-full daily vitamin organizer with omega-3 fish oil, which promises to enhance memory and tastes exactly as you would expect.

I have a friend who begins her reminiscences by saying, "In the summer of 1974," and admire how she can make such precise distinctions. I can identify the big events: Deaths. Graduations. Divorces. Love affairs—their beginnings and endings. But the in-between years of my life have blurred, their distinct ingredients no longer readily identifiable. I've saved all my datebooks since 1978, and while some startling memories surface on their pages, they're also littered with names and events I don't remember. People with whom I apparently spent a good deal of time. Why was I meeting Amy for lunch so often? Did I even like her? If so, why is she gone? What and who has replaced her? My friend is amazing with dates, but not as agile with names. When she meets someone she ought to know but doesn't, she smiles broadly and says, "Hello, you." I haven't tried that one yet.

Remembering and forgetting collide when I begin a story and spot the glazed expression on the face of my listener, becoming ashamedly aware that this is one they've heard before. Perhaps many times before. They're kind and pretend this isn't a repetition, and I'm embarrassed and wind down as quickly as I gracefully can. I don't say, "Stop me if you've heard this," because I'm not prepared to acknowledge that my repetition is as frequent as I fear it has become. I guess being willing to say that dreaded phrase will be my next step, if only as an act of kindness to my friends whose patience with my voluble longwindedness is gratefully appreciated. And, of course, as an act of self-protectiveness for me.

As I complete this piece, I am one month post major surgery and beginning to sense that forgetting has decided advantages. There is relief in being unable to summon up the precise experience of being in a recovery room pressing the tightly clenched button for pain relief or being awakened for CT scans at 3:00 a.m. Years ago, the surgeon who did my knee replacement assured me that the pain I'd experience would be like childbirth. He was right. I don't remember the pain, just that there was a lot of it. My recent surgery and hospital stay have begun to drift out to the edges of memory, becoming an accumulation of accounts I tell my friends. Hopefully not repeatedly. I'm happy to let those memories go.

There is still enough fullness in my mind to allow me the freedom to throw at least most of my emptiness to the winds. But since my throwing arm is limited by an arthritic shoulder, I imagine flinging all of it—proper nouns, my inability to hold on to the thread of a story if I reach for embellishment, and remembering the wrong things—into the back of my kitchen catchall drawer. There they will come to rest along with the half-burned birthday candles, chopsticks from long-ago take-out orders, and my mother's tarnished silver nutcracker. I'll go forward with whatever memory remains, buttressed by a game or two and my omega-3 fish oil. That, and the comfort that my friends are as old as I am. And if their memory is a little better, their hearing is a little worse. Navigating our retracting dendrites and shrinking neurons has become a collective enterprise.

PASSWORDS

I'm comfortably perched at my computer, a hot coffee to my left, a toasted English muffin to my right, and between them, the assortment of morning supplements that accompany both. I open my most recent draft of this collection and await a stroke of literary brilliance to descend upon me.

Instead, an alert that I'm running out of space pops up. Certain that can't be the case, I delete it, but it re-appears on my screen at one-minute intervals to my increasing impatience, then growing alarm.

I settle in to solve this undoubtedly minor issue. No problem, my "Manage this icon" menu assures me. Move what you don't need to iCloud where it will live until you want it. With relief, I go to my applications folder and highlight everything that I probably won't use ever again in a million years, but you never know.

I'll just tuck them into or onto the cloud—however one tucks in relation to a cloud.

Instead, I face a spinning wheel on my screen, which happens, my godson has explained in that painstaking way young boys speak to old women, "when the computer is thinking." I am waiting for it to figure out whatever it needs to and get me to where I want to go.

But, as I attempt this transfer, I'm asked for the password for my applications. No problem. I'll cycle through my primary passwords, sure that one of them will succeed. But they don't. I turn to my list of printed-out special passwords, those that required adding a symbol or number to one of my familiar phrases. Nope.

Passwords seem so obvious and rememberable when I create them. My childhood home address. My daughters' nicknames. Book titles. Bits and pieces of information I have carried with me all my life. They're locked into my brain. Until they're not.

I turn to my old friend magical thinking. Perhaps I misspelled the password. *I was in a hurry,* I tell myself. This will turn out to be as uncomplicated as an unwitting typo. I take a deep breath, repeat every street name, nickname, author—to no avail. Not even a drop of avail. No new window opens, leading me down another, possibly more successful line of technological inquiry. Just the same dogged insistence on my application password.

I google "how do I find my application password?"

and am informed thusly: I should be looking for the "16-character code in the yellow bar" and that I should only have to enter it once. Google even tells me not to worry about memorizing it.

The problem here is that there is no yellow bar on my device.

I restart the machine again, have another cup of coffee. I can do this. I have to do this. I walk around trying to think of something I haven't thought of yet. Perhaps instead of an entire application that I appear clearly unable to move, I'll come at this in smaller increments. Not big files, but bits and pieces of files that will eventually add up to make the space I need.

I spend the next hour going through my music, which takes up the biggest category of content. Am I ever really going to listen to Buddy Guy again? Or the Commodores? I begin to delete, making my way up through the *Hs*, then with renewed hope, check the system folder to see how much room I have created. None. Removing one album at a time is clearly not the way forward.

I try YouTube. There's a YouTube for everything, and it's been a successful resource for me in the past. But in order to get the right video, you must ask a precise question. "How do I get this goddamn stuff off my computer, either into the garbage forever or resting comfortably in the cloud?" isn't succinct enough.

Eventually I find one that I hope is in simple-enough English for me to understand. The young man (why are they always young men?) explains, and explains, until I realize I've lost track of where we are. Some of it is his language, which appears to be made up of letters and numbers instead of words.

It starts off inviting enough: "To move applications to the cloud, there are options available." Perfect. But as he describes the options, the means of accomplishing them use tools that don't sound real: IaaS, PaaS, SaaS. (I learn later those refer to infrastructure-as-a-service, platform-as-a-service, and software-as-a-service.) He talks about bitmaps, persistent states, encryption, device identifiers, and account tokens. There are graphics designed, I'm sure, to be illuminating, but I don't understand what is being illuminated. Nor do I understand what I'm watching on this video. But while I'm already on YouTube, I take a little break and watch an Alicia Keys video, which lifts my spirits a bit and strengthens my stubborn resolve to be triumphant over this piece of impenetrable technology.

I open the keychain application that contains all my passwords. There is no category called "applications," although the way into every hotel, airport, organization, and magazine subscription is there, all neatly alphabetized. Now, not only am I irritable given the interminable hours I've spent with this uncompromising machine, but I'm disappointed in my own inability to figure this out. I have 5.66 GB out of 250 GB left. Whether that's a good GB number or not, I have made a tremendous mess. My cloud is cluttered with applications, documents, email correspondence, and individual songs. My photographs must be hidden somewhere. My nerves are shot.

With both resignation and guilty relief, I call my computer repair guy. I don't say, in a high whiny voice, "I don't know what's wrong. I don't know what I did to make it worse. Please erase what I did, find the error, and fix it." I have my dignity. As I begin to explain what is wrong, I hear the desperation creeping into my voice and begin to make less and less sense, even to myself.

He interrupts and says soothingly, "Why don't you drop it off? I'll take a look and do whatever kung fu is needed." Kung fu? Really? Is that what is called for here? I was hoping for a more high-tech kind of answer. Is he being dismissively ageist or warmly reassuring? I like and trust him, martial arts references notwithstanding, so the clogged-up computer is relievedly deposited to his care.

Two days later, he calls to tell me everything is fixed and ready for pickup. When I arrive, using my most well-informed voice, I ask him to explain what went wrong.

"It appears that your log expanded to the amount of available GB space," he says.

I know that already and ask him why that happened,

imagining an amoeba-like substance filling up all available crevices inside my computer.

"It would be like if a stenographer had come into your house," he explains—I know then he is purposely choosing his words because that's an entirely old-lady reference. The generations that have followed mine probably don't even know what a stenographer is— "copied everything you've ever written, and stored it in the log."

I feel both stupid and annoyed with him, and still don't know what my log is, so I switch the focus.

"Did you need the application password to fix everything?" I ask. "If not, why was the computer asking for one?"

He says something like I wandered down the wrong electronic road and the application password wouldn't have gotten me where I needed to go anyway. That's where I lose him, so I smile, my authoritative dignity in tatters.

This precise moment of losing the explanatory thread is echoed whenever my car needs a repair. I understand the need for gas, oil changes, tire rotation, and regular service. But when the mechanic begins to use words like *crankshaft*, I thank him (still mostly hims) and pay my bill. I don't need to understand everything. I don't even need to understand most things. I'm good with what I already know. And none of it involves the inner workings of either cars or computers.

I return home, grateful for my computer now brimming with hundreds and hundreds of GBs ready to be pressed into service. I still don't know what went wrong or what he did to stop it from recurring.

My grandmother used to unplug all the light fixtures before she left her apartment because "you never know what might happen." She was right. Not only will I never know what is going to happen, even when it happens, but without asking for help, I won't be able to make it stop happening. Words to live by. My grandmother's name is my new password.

NEW MATH FOR
AN OLD WOMAN

The media presents me, a denizen of the world of the old, with two possibilities that describe how this time is likely to unfold. The first is illuminated in a ubiquitous television commercial featuring a blond middle-aged woman looking solemn and concerned and talking directly to the sons and daughters (but, of course, mostly the daughters) of moms everywhere.

What's best for Mom, she chirps, when she can't keep up her home any longer? When she can no longer drive the family car? When she confuses her medications or forgets to take them entirely? There is a pause then to let the severity of these questions sink in, after which she proposes a range of services that will assist the viewer in accessing the necessary resources and products for their newly errant mom. What is missing from this equation is . . . wait for it . . . Mom.

The alternative representations are in magazines featuring mostly white women with startlingly unlined skin—on their faces, arms, and legs—smiling broadly as they play a round of golf, extol the benefits of their exercise routines, or display their newly developed skill of baking or potting. None of these women have glaucoma, thinning hair, or orthopedic shoes, unless it's in an ad to sell remedies for their eyes, their hair, or their feet.

These appear to be my disheartening choices: I can either dedicate myself to remaining upbeat, plucky, and ever improving, or sink into slow doddering decline and eventual need of management by my daughters.

None of that is true, either of me or of nearly any of the old women I know. I have never baked or knitted, and it is unlikely that they will serve as vocabularies of self-expression for me now.

I'm aware that my driving increasingly drifts toward the slow right lane on the freeway, but I'm confident I'll be able to recognize when it's time to stop driving—first in the rain, then at night, then entirely—before I come to the same unceremonious end of my driving career as my mother did when she rear-ended a police car.

I have three grab bars in my bathroom and move around in the watery space with my full attention. When I go for a walk, I remain alert to roots, stones over which I might trip, potholes into which I might stumble, my once-easy, unthinking stride a thing of the past. I keep my phone with me all the time now—just in case.

It's not that I don't know I'm old. After all, I'm old all day long. I know it better than anyone, know exactly the forms it takes and the adaptations I need to make to accommodate it.

There is math involved in my life now, but not the measurements of a gerontological life stage. For those who study oldness, there are the young-old—the freshmen at aging. They're between sixty-five and seventy-five. Then there are those who are counted as full-fledged old, spanning seventy-five to eighty-five. That's me. Then for those who graduate from old, there are the old-old. That group begins at eighty-five and lasts until they no longer do. But what the dominant culture expects of and from us oldies is both disheartening and disrespectful. Not for me. I don't want to be categorized and counted. I'll be my own counter.

Upon awakening, I count how many hours I have slept. I am a "good sleeper" and know the number of hours my body needs. Ideally. But there are the nights I'm ruminating about something, or excited about something else, or I ate too much watermelon or the whole bag of pistachio nuts. Then the hours are just barely adequate to navigate the next day. When I was in fourth grade, I got a C– in citizenship. I was just barely managing as a good citizen. Sometimes, I just barely get along on not enough sleep. Those are C– nights.

I count the number of steps I take each day. I incrementally increase goals for myself, and my sense of pride lasts for the entire day when I reach them. Occasionally, I combine both the steps and the speed at which I take them and imagine my heart smiling at me as it pumps away, appreciative that I am paying such responsible attention to it. My cell phone does a lot of the counting for me, and I track my number, trying to get at least to the five thousand mark, but proud of myself when I get up to seven or eight thousand. Like I get an A in walking.

Then there's counting my medicines. There are actual drugs my body needs because I have "conditions" that require them. I take as few of those as possible. Supplements are another matter. I take a lot of letters. B, C, D, and E. Some that presumably help memory. But so far, it's only with the help of secret notes that I've managed not to leave friends waiting for me on street corners. Well, just that once. But she was understanding about it.

I have a two-week plastic pill container with big letters identifying the day in question, and each section is filled with my weekly medications and relevant supplements. I need a two-week container and my mother's cloisonné pillbox for one week because many of my supplement capsules are enormous. I'm not sure why.

Perhaps companies imagine size signals effectiveness. So I count, carefully place each pill in its designated home, and each morning take out the correct number that will hopefully augment my health and well-being.

Not calories though. I haven't counted those in fifty years. I maintain what I consider to be a well-balanced diet, although not necessarily within each meal, or even each day. What I'm going for is that by the end of the week, I've achieved a semblance of balance.

The day-by-day effort goes like this: A big, buttery, creamy bowl of pasta with bacon, cheese, and sweet peas for dinner one day is balanced with a large green salad dressed with an austere squeeze of lemon the next. A double scoop of ice cream with berries and a shortbread cookie for dessert lead to sliced apples with a little sprinkle of cinnamon. The week-by-week effort is more me deciding how many days in a row I can eat excessively before reining myself in and replacing what I'm eating with food that is healthier for me. I suppose you could make the case that what I do is an elaborate way of counting calories, but my way works for me and allows me to imagine that I have a relaxed and flexible attitude toward food.

I count my money. All the time. There is a fixed amount that has to last as long as I last. But I could last longer. If I last shorter, that's OK because my kids will get the difference. But if not, the kids will have to spend their old-age money on my old age. I hope that doesn't happen. But it might. And they'd be willing. But I wouldn't. I keep careful track of my money.

I read the obits every day to acknowledge the deaths of the iconic cultural, literary, and political figures who have shaped my world. Then I check their ages. Too young to die is anyone younger than I am. Deaths of those about my age elicit sorrow, and those who have lived into their nineties leave me with envy and a little hope. But all of them are counted.

Finally, 5:00 p.m. is still and has always been the end of the workday, even though I haven't worked from nine to five in a very long time. I still remember relievedly placing the cover over my typewriter, clearing off my desk, and getting ready to go home from the offices that supported me and my daughters for decades. That was when I poured a drink, a reward for having made it through another day. But eventually I stopped drinking, because the one drink at five grew to two before dinner, then another one after, then the numbers expanded, and my life contracted. But five still marks the time when I no longer must be productive. Or keep track of anything. The day is over, and I don't need to begin again till tomorrow morning. I read, I listen to music, I look out the window and daydream. I do what I did when I was twelve and didn't know there would ever come a time when I would be an old woman who counts.

MY FINAL REPORT CARD

My television set sits atop a low filing cabinet, and one afternoon, needing to find some way to manage my growing anxiety while watching the ominous evening news, I decided to create a new and improved filing system during the commercial breaks. In the process, I stumbled upon my fourth-grade report card, inexplicably filed in "Home Improvement 2009."

In 1946, report cards were sent home for parents' signatures and represented the quarterly assessment of how well students were progressing. Each subject was defined by letters (A through F) accompanied by numbers (1 through 5). The letter reflected the quality of scholarship displayed, and the number identified the budding student's class participation. Even when I earned an A or a B in a subject, I got a lot of 3s due to not raising my hand and enthusiastically waving it around, trying to show the teacher how much I knew. Also, I probably talked too much. This turned out to be an accurate foreshadowing of both my intellectual and behavioral life.

Reading was, and has always been, my intellectual strength. Reading, and writing, talking about reading and writing, then doing it some more. I loved all of it.

Getting my first library card the day after my sixth birthday, I made my painstaking choice of the six permitted books for that week. I felt a personal sense of accomplishment when the librarian placed a firm and decisive stamp identifying the necessary return date on the cards placed inside little envelopes glued to the backs of the books.

I read indiscriminately, hungry for stories about other boys and girls, children who lived in houses where everyone smiled, had adventures, and never felt sad or scared. I was Nancy Drew all the way. Of course, Nancy didn't have a mother, which made my imaginative flights so much easier. Only a doting father and her own convertible. I was going to be her, just as soon as I got bigger.

By the time my fourth-grade report card was issued, I had progressed to reading and writing book reports that were about both the plot and my opinion about how well I thought the author had written it. In the fifth and sixth grades, books assigned for English class were identified as classics. They were mostly boring, but I didn't mind because each was only one of the eight or ten books I read every week. By seventh grade I was placed in an advanced class where we read Dickens and other heartbreaking authors. Grammatical rules, sentence structure, and other fundamentals were not part of the advanced curriculum. I suppose the teachers imagined we would pick up the basics by osmosis. But I never did, and my semicolons are invariably misplaced, my prepositions are scattered about in no particular order, and my ability to parse a sentence beyond subject, verb, predicate is a decided flunk.

So instead of the A1 I want to give myself, because of my grammatical limitations I'll make it a B1 in English. Not reading. I still read voraciously, and sinking into a skillful, graceful, and compelling use of language to tell a story has been one of the greatest pleasures of my life. If there were a prize for best reader, I would get it.

In 1946, history was the white story of the world, with America at the center. There were a lot of wars to learn, dates of declarations, and explanations of men doing things brave or horrible, depending on what side they were on. All I needed to do was memorize the battles, the treaties, and the cities and countries in which the wars were waged to get good grades on the tests—and on flash quizzes if the teacher was sneaky. But history didn't become real to me until I overheard whispered conversations between my mother and her parents about the Holocaust. This was history, and it was happening right now, not in a long-ago century. Over the decades that followed, I began to understand that the wars and their outcomes were written by their winners. Increasingly, the heroes and villains of my textbooks shifted as scholars revealed and rewrote the canon of my childhood. So, for history, I give myself an A1 for what was compulsory then and another A1 for what was more essential in life.

Geography was once, like history, entirely memorization. Africa was the Dark Continent, and there was not much known about it. People who lived in other faraway places were considered to be exotic; we studied their food and clothing and learned the name of the man who was in charge of the country. Now, over a half century later, there is a field of study called the politics of geography, to which feminists have brought their own lens. Space. Who creates the borders where space begins and ends? What are the resources within the space and how they are utilized—and by whom? I love geography now and can still, if needed (which it never is), recite the names of most of the state capitals. Another A1.

The next category will undoubtedly be unfamiliar to readers under sixty-five, but penmanship was once considered its own subject. We learned the Palmer method and practiced writing letters on lined pages, both in cursive and print, until each stroke was as exact as that required of a Torah scribe. In high school, shorthand was offered as a second language for girls who were planning to enter the workforce after high school. Girls planning to go to college didn't have to take it.

There have been many times I wished I had less training in Palmer handwriting and more knowledge about shorthand, given that the notes I take in meetings are usually illegible. My class privilege kept me from a skill I might have functionally used. I didn't learn bookkeeping either. I suppose the thinking in the 1940s and early 1950s was that I would never have to take minutes or dictation or manage money. I give myself a grade that declines with my age. My penmanship is a C sliding into a D, especially when I'm in a hurry. But for most of my life, it was a B sliding into a C. My number? An impatient 3.

Then there was gym. I was terrible at gym. Really, embarrassingly awful. First of all, there were the gym suits that displayed everything that was wrong with everyone's bodies. Our gangling arms and legs jutted out from the coarse cotton uniforms we changed into before class. Then, exposed and awkward, we had to climb ropes that hung from the ceiling with knots at foot-long intervals. The task was to climb the knots to the ceiling and triumphantly holler, announcing our accomplishment to all the students assembled below on the glistening floor of the gym. The supergood athletes were able to climb without knots, but the regular kids, which were most of us, needed the extra help. I was a skinny bookish girl and invariably let go after reaching as far as the second knot, just two feet from the floor.

My legs were long though, and I was excellent on the pommel horse, holding the saddle handles and swinging my legs easily over the top, an athletic skill that, except for mounting and dismounting horses, didn't ever translate into anything else.

I intermittently joined and dropped out of gyms over the decades, and continue to find exercise tiresome, sweaty, and unpleasant. I walk most days now, do what I pretend is yoga but is really stretching, and that's it. I have been blessed with a body that has withstood my excessive drinking, smoking, and lack of attention to good nutrition until the last two decades and has still managed, with a couple of temporary exceptions, to function very well. So, all in all, the gym grade on my life's report card would be a C4.

There's arithmetic. I'm pretty basic there and got good grades all the way up to geometry and algebra's substitution. My grade plummeted when I started to wear a girdle to contain thighs that were too big and rubbed against one another when I walked. Geometry period was 11:10 to 11:50 a.m., and by then my rubber constraints began to slowly roll up my legs and dig into my groin, which is really all I remember about geometry. Girdles and groin pain. I might have done better if I'd had smaller thighs or didn't think they had to be contained. Now I understand that the symbols were gateways to problem-solving and logic, metaphors for a larger conceptual idea, but then, in high school, I was watching the clock, waiting for the end of class so I could run to the bathroom and pull the legs of my girdle down.

I have successfully continued to manage the arithmetic part of adult life. I keep a precise checkbook and learned to make and use spreadsheets when that became possible on my computer. I'm up to date with basic math. So I'd give myself a lifetime B2 in arithmetic and an F4 in anything more complex.

As I moved into preadolescence (not even identified as a subcategory of human development at that time), I took homemaking, which included the two stalwarts, sewing and cooking. I succeeded pretty well with the running stitch, only occasionally sticking a needle into my finger when trying to thread it and getting a little drop of blood on the white burlap we used. Not often, but enough to drop my grade.

Once we moved away from the basic running stitch to the more complex blanket or chain stitch, I fell behind. Quickly. I could do a cross-stitch, which meant I was relegated to a piece of cotton with a homiletic saying or picture of a colonial girl that I would fill in to make a sampler. That was the high point of my sewing.

It's not like I don't have a legacy. My grandfather was a master tailor, the guy who put white chalk marks on the suits of the gangsters and successful businessmen who bought them at Crawford Clothing on Broadway in the 1930s and '40s. My mother never sewed. There was always a big straw laundry basket of clothes that needed buttons replaced or hems altered waiting for my grandfather when he came to visit. I don't know whether it was her way of feeling taken care of by her father, or if sewing didn't fit with her carefully practiced ideas of assimilation. But it wasn't a part of my life. Except for the samplers that mercifully have been lost along the way. Sewing grade: D4.

Then cooking. In the early 1950s, there was a singular emphasis on this being a valuable life path for women. Tens of thousands had gone to work in factories and offices in the name of the war effort and needed to be recontained in their homes, so advertisements in magazines and on the radio touted scientific ways of cooking and the use of modern home appliances. Garbage disposals, freezers, dishwashers, and pressure cookers were designed to allow women more leisure time, even as the standards and expectations of cleanliness and elaborate food preparation skyrocketed. The advertised goal of having time to sit down and read a ladies' magazine was rarely the outcome.

I learned to cook with the revolutionary invention of cake mixes. "Just add an egg and some water and it's done!" the ads proclaimed. Even a ten-year-old could make dessert in this brave new world. But I simply didn't find preparing food as interesting as reading books. Left to my own devices, reading was always the first choice. My homemaking grade, then and now, is a C with an accompanying number of 4.

We conclude my report card with what was initially my worst grade. Citizenship. I just couldn't seem to get along. I didn't understand that there were expectations about how girls should relate to authority figures, values about the importance of feminine propriety and maintaining a pleasant demeanor, institutional requirements that determined classroom decorum. I just knew that I was a barely average citizen, which hurt my feelings because I didn't know why and was unable to ask. Grades were simply given, but they were never questioned. Decades later, I suspect it meant I asked too many questions. Teachers were authorities in their subjects, and students asked questions to be sure they understood what had been said, not to challenge it.

When I was a child and asked my grandfather a question, he always responded in the same way: "On the one hand . . ." And then he answered the question I posed. Then he would continue, "But on the other hand . . ." and provide another possible answer. "But on the other hand," he went on, and in this way proposed answer upon answer upon answer, possibility upon possibility for my curious mind.

Only much later did I understand that asking questions was a part of my Jewish legacy. There were no answers, my grandfather taught me by graceful indirection, only better questions. I finally became a good citizen. A really good citizen. A1 for me.

But a report card needs a parent's signature. Since I no longer have any, I've decided my mother would sign off on the grades I've assigned myself, then say she'd have given me all A1s as a daughter and as a person. That would be the best report card of all.

BUT WHAT ABOUT MY JOURNALS?

The worn mesh bag had split open, and ping-pong balls rolled all over the floor, under the sofa, and into the kitchen. This is the last straw. I have too much stuff.

I'd ordered the set of ping-pong paddles and balls when I was teaching my then young godson to play. They came in packages of twenty-four, which was twenty-two more than I needed, so I left them in their original container. We played every time he came to visit until he could easily beat me, at which point he lost interest.

Now they are all over my floor. I understand this rolling emergency as an alarm bell signaling the time for me to release all my unnecessary excess. Besides the errant ping-pong balls, there are the unintelligible collections of papers, objects collected on vacations, broken appliances I've never gotten around to fixing, faded wrapping paper, and all the unrelated detritus that is stuffed into the back of my closets. I don't want my daughters to have to pick their way through a lot of accumulated clutter to find something of sentimental value after my death. I want to do that for them. It's intended to be a kind of after-the-fact gift. That's the plan, anyhow. I'll winnow and let go of all my chaff. I'm too old for chaff. All that accumulation is a young person's game. I want to strip everything down to the heart of the matter. The heart of what matters to me.

My first step requires identifying the wheat I want for my personal field and what can be thrown out. I'll discard the latter, rearrange the former, and temporarily store whatever I still can't decide on. As a plan, it seems straightforward.

I begin, as I do in most things, with my mother. After the more than eighteen years since her death, I stack her multiple sets of dishes and the wooden box containing her ornate sterling silver on my dining room table, along with nine vases, four tablecloths, six red-and-white wine glasses, and two large serving platters; divide everything evenly; and prepare to mail them to my daughters. They are in a time of their lives where these objects carry both personal memory and practical usefulness.

I keep her cloisonné pillbox and use it for my

morning supplements, beginning my day by opening the small decorative case, imagining our hands briefly brushing together. She kept her mother's monogrammed fancy handkerchief (not for blowing) nestled at the bottom of her handbag; when she changed handbags, it too was transferred. As was my pillbox.

I fill cartons with clothes I thought I'd wear but rarely do and donate them. I give books I'll never read again to the local high school library. Beach towels—I don't go to the beach anymore—pool noodles, and rafts from when my godson was a baby. A camping coffee maker. A travel iron. Feeling lighter with each decision, I ruthlessly make my way through closets, drawers, even the trunk of my car. I give up the woven basket held as a memory of a long-ago weekend romance and bowls of too many shells and stones from hundreds of walks on the beach.

My wheat and chaff are fairly straightforward. But then I collide against objects that are not quite either one, but rather representations of my history. A chipped pottery jug from a trip to Mexico with friends that occasionally holds dried flowers. Three menorahs, only one of which I find beautiful. Candlesticks I've never used, and those I've tired of. These artifacts represent decades of ceremonies and holidays, and as my eyes fall on them lying disregarded on the shelf behind my cleaning supplies, I remember the gatherings they illuminated, the blessings that were offered over their flames. They hold my past, and with my memory aging along with the rest of me, they're unused but still reliable prompts. I decide to make chaff-adjacent its own category and will return to it every year to reassess.

Then I create my personal attic by emptying the top shelf of my linen closet. When I was young, there was a cord hanging from the second-floor hallway ceiling of our home that, when tugged with all the force of my child self, folded down into a ladder I could climb to a magical repository of old steamer trunks, hatboxes, a Persian lamb muff, a toboggan, and a partial chess set. Resting in a corner on pink insulation material were my father's pipes and mother's cigarette box. All portals to an earlier time.

Now that I have my own attic, I gather up my daughters' elementary school photos, high school and college satin graduation robes, birthday cards, diplomas, and letters. My father's driver's license, his shoehorn with its graceful ivory handle, and the home movies he made from inside the plane as it took off and landed in 1944, so proud to be among the first air travelers. Browning photos of immigrant ancestors, my mother's once-creamy, now-cracked ivory leather gloves. My brother's tallit.

In the corner, under the reading light, rests my once-splendid green leather La-Z-Boy, which swivels and reclines (me too) and holds my body perfectly. She's big and puffy (so am I), and I've loved her every single day of the thirty years we've spent together. But, like me, she's in decline. Random pumpkin seeds have permanently disappeared after being caught in her deep crevices. Her color has faded, scratches and dings are scattered across the arms, and stuffing peeks through splitting seams. She has been, without a doubt, the most comfortable chair I've ever owned, but she's nearly all worn out now and squeaks when she swivels. It's just a little squeak, like a weak protest from an old lady trying to climb a flight of stairs while her children are watching, wanting to seem indefatigable; her legs would squeak in protest, if they could.

I feel guilty now that all I see are her flaws. She's stretched out and faded, like me. And I want a shinier, newer model. I worry that I've turned into one of those men who marry younger versions of their wives as soon as they begin to show their age. I'm ashamed I can't settle into the comfortable joining of my old bottom and the shapeless seat of my chair, but I want a perky bottom with springs that spring. Yet my decision to cast her off, after so many years of devoted service, feels judgy and dismissive.

Decades ago, during an earlier attempt at winnowing, I made a fatal mistake with my music library. After being first shamed, then convinced that I was entirely behind the times and that CDs were the most acoustically pristine way to listen to music, I traded in my years of carefully collected records—33⅓s and 45s—and tapes. Everything in my eclectic and extensive library had skips and scratches, hisses and water- or wine-stained covers. Each blemish marked the precise spot where years of repetitively playing and replaying one track over and over and over had left their mark. Chet Baker playing "My Funny Valentine" was practically ruined. But so was I during the years I listened to it and relived the love affair that it represented. Marvin Gaye's "What's Going On" was a political anthem repeated into blurriness. John Coltrane's *A Love Supreme* had seven skips, and I knew when each one was coming and prepared for it. They had become part of the music. And, of course, everything that Carmen McRae ever recorded was what I'll politely call "lived in."

CDs became the substitute for my beloved assortment of records and tapes, and while it is true that the sound is entirely flawless, my music sounds like a face lifted of all its well-earned and lived-in wrinkles. The hisses and skips during either songs about love affairs that ended badly or those that lent themselves to an animated improvisational dance when I was alone are now absent. I don't want my music to be perfect. I want it to be lived in. Like me. I miss my LPs and wish I had kept them. I don't want to mistakenly discard my old chair like I had my records and need to find a way to keep her. Somewhere.

My youngest (yet late-middle-aged) daughter has a

spare room, and we agree that my chair will continue her aging there, placed in anticipation of my occasional visits. I replace her with a new, unfamiliarly firm, and supple chair. She is butterscotch leather and does everything. She swivels, rocks, and tilts back and is padded, soft, and inviting. My current experience of kicking up my heels is watching my feet rise as the chair reclines.

But this glorious sparkling leather chair isn't going to retain her newness. She too will display signs of spills, scratches, and dings. Already there's a bright red Sharpie mark on the arm, her first permanent stain. I suspect there are already a couple of sesame seeds in its folds and maybe one black bean, all beyond my reach. We're companionably settling in together, the two of us.

As my eyes sweep across the expanse of my living room and study, I am soothed, rooted, held by my wheat. So far, so good. I feel lighter and have vacuumed my newly spacious closets and dusted the shelves where there is now a spot for a picture or plant between my remaining books. I've given away, pared down, sorted, and organized and am left with my well-worn, comfortable, sufficient landscape. What remains is my painstakingly curated mature wheat. I know the origin story of every remaining object in my home. There are gifts I delight in and those that remain in the shadowy recesses of the closet until the cherished woman with dubious taste comes to visit. A sculpture of my eldest daughter, then in her early thirties, leg extended, arms upraised, dancing. My shofar and Shabbat candlesticks. A woven cup my beloved and I bought at a craft fair thirty-five years ago, in the time before she began to die. The wooden tables in my living room with their rings from unattended glasses, mugs, and overwatered plants—faithful reminders of all the years, the conversations, the laughter that those stains represent. We have a long and companionable history, and I keep them well polished, heightening their lustrous discolorations. My graceful but faded curtains that blend compatibly with the rest of the room, even my impulse purchase of a dramatic oxblood-colored stone lamp that never shed useful light resides, impressive and unlit, on a side table.

But . . . what about my journals? They date back to 1978, and discarding them would make me feel like I'm already dead. What would be ideal is for them to magically evaporate at the precise moment of my last breath, but that's not going to happen. I have to decide.

I'm not a famous woman who leaves behind journals that allow an eventual biographer to more deeply plumb the inner recesses of my thinking and prodigious output. Everything I wanted to write and send into the world is already out there. These are bread crumbs leading back to my younger self to whom everything mattered so much.

These journals are a record of how I navigated the

life of my past self, her vulnerabilities, and her carefully constructed defenses as she moved into and through middle age. I read them and remember the collisions with the deaths that shaped her, her explosions of judgment, impatience, insecurity, and loneliness. Read how she clung to the outcomes she was certain were what she needed and wanted. I don't want to lose her. Destroying these journals is an act of silencing and erasure. And I feel so tenderly toward her; I want to put my arms around this earnest scribbler.

But ours is a private relationship, not one to be shared with my daughters. I don't want them to see the written proof of my judgments about their choices, my conflicts about being a mother, and how they collided with my hunger to be in the world. It won't be a surprise to them, of course. But it will be indelible. And consequently, I imagine, deeply painful. No eyes but mine can understand the genesis of these words, and I can't bring myself to get rid of any of it. Not yet.

Once or twice a year, I move my private writings from the apartment to my storage unit where I slide the box of notebooks, flash drives, calendars, and random jottings next to my collection of canes, crutches from my knee replacements, and my—just in case of emergencies—walker. This is intended as a first step toward moving them into the trunk of my car and finally releasing their contents to a shredder. But within months, sometimes even sooner, I bring them all back into the apartment, not ready to erase the record of my history nor have it moldering in a cluttered bin with health equipment, my first wedding album, and the artificially colorized infant photos of me and my brother. Right now, the box is in the back of the front hall closet, behind my winter coats.

Now, when the political world overwhelms me, or a close friend is ill, or my daughters are navigating their lives and I fight the impulse to instruct them about exactly how the navigation should proceed, I putter. Nothing significant is ever accomplished. The kitchen drawer that has accumulated string for tying chicken legs, pushpins, matchbooks, two old skewers, plastic ties, three baggies, and a nutcracker is properly sorted. My shoes are reordered on the closet floor, sandals at the back, sneakers on the side, and everyday oxfords in the front. Plants are repotted and pens that have died are buried.

When I finish, everything looks just as it had when I began, but I'm filled with a sense of satisfaction and accomplishment that in no way mirrors what has just taken place. Sitting in my new chair, surrounded by my beloved wheat, having discarded the chaff and stuffed the remainder into the ever-changing margins of my newly created attic, I have come to rest. Except, of course, for the journals.

TILL DEATH DO US PART

Obit Draft

BUTLER, Wallace, age 9_ of Phoenix, Arizona, died . . . He is survived by his three daughters, grandson, and great-granddaughter.

He was a graduate of Northwestern University and a World War II veteran, and delighted in his life in New York, where he owned one of the last letterpress printing shops. A lover of Sinatra, golf, and martinis, he was a devoted husband, proud father, and dependable friend. He was a romantic, and his third marriage was the charm. This thirty-five-year partnership was filled with travel, theater, and entertaining. An owner of cats and a lover of animals, he was a contributor to the ASPCA and enjoyed volunteering at the Central Park Zoo. As he aged, his fundamental adaptability was evident in his move to Phoenix, where he could be close to his daughters and enjoy the pleasures of a very different city.

Memorial services will be held at Sinai Mortuary (address, date, and time).

My daughters and I drafted this obituary for the dying man who was once my husband. He and I weren't married very long or very successfully, but we had two children together, daughters who are now in late middle age. Since his move from New York to Phoenix, he calls to wish me a happy Mother's Day, thanking me for being such a good mother to them. I wasn't all that good, but he is generous, much as he was as a father and husband.

He hates organized religion and show-offs, and loves baseball, Ava Gardner, and melancholy violin music. He still drinks too much and repeats himself, which he did even before he grew old. He is not a man I could have spent my feminist life with.

I retrieve my 1956 wedding album from the cobwebby recesses of the storage unit. Everyone on its yellowing pages is dead; there is no one left who knew us then. We both imagined everything would be ahead of us and that we might escape the undertow of our family legacies, he under the dominating control of a successful and demanding immigrant father and I chafing under the manicured thumb of an equally controlling and ambitious mother.

I study my face arranged for all the prescribed poses of the wedding album form: walking down the aisle with my father; feeding my previously married, thirty-three-year-old husband a piece of wedding cake; dancing a carefully practiced rhumba, our first dance. But I cannot remember myself. At eighteen, I was playing my role in a highly scripted event where everyone but me seemed to know their part.

There was one child, then another; an apartment, then a large brick home; one car, then two; more and more belongings to dust and wash, arrange and display. According to both our parents' standards at least, we were reassuringly successful.

Our marriage operated within the division of roles common in white middle-class marriages of the mid-1950s. He went to work outside, and I went to work inside, mothering, cooking, cleaning, organizing our social life, and seeing that everything ran as smoothly as possible. There was always a drink and dinner waiting at the end of his day, after which he played with the girls for a while. Then I took them upstairs for bath-and bedtime so he could relax after his workday, which was assumed to be more demanding than my own. We

drank together, his multiple martinis and my overea-
ger whiskey sours; shared the ongoing dramas of our
siblings, in-laws, and friends; and navigated domestic
details and those of our bed, until the cultural realities
that defined 1956 became the radically altered landscape of 1963.

That summer, drawn by the growing urgencies
of the civil rights movement, I joined the March on
Washington for Jobs and Freedom. I was awakening
to the realities of American injustice and had begun
to study the words of writers and musicians I admired,
apprenticing myself to their ideas. Nina Simone at the
Village Gate singing "Mississippi Goddam." James
Baldwin fiercely trying to explain to white people the
danger we were all in. Before the march, the assassina-
tion of Medgar Evers. After it, that of President Kennedy.

My carefully curated suburban life felt increasingly
like a premature compromise, and I wanted to be in the
middle of things. Wherever that meant. By the end of
that year, I had left my marriage, having no idea what
that might require of me.

I left him hurt and wounded as I gathered our
daughters, fleeing into what I imagined would be our
exhilarating new future. It wasn't, of course. It was
simply a life like all lives, requiring a different set of
choices, necessary compromises, inevitable losses, and
unexpected opportunities.

I began as a divorced, newly emerging leftie but by

the end of that decade became an exuberant feminist, leaving both the Old and the New Left behind. After meeting the woman who became my great love, I lived for a decade as a lesbian-feminist activist, engaged in the effort to end violence against women, then after her death a lesbian-feminist widow and writer. Now I am an old woman who carries all those identities—and more.

Over all that time, I rarely thought about him or our years together. He represented a part of my life that held too many guilty memories that I papered over with a well-crafted critique about the damages of patriarchal institutions, the constricting nature of conventional marriage, and all the ways it's propped up by women's unpaid labor. While all of that was true, my analysis was a self-protective one, serving to shield me from any sense of discomfort about my part in why our life together had ended.

He was, at least according to our daughters, happy. They didn't like his new wife, of course. Or her daughter. Or that he had chosen them. But they appeared at all the necessary celebrations and birthdays, keeping me up to date on the labyrinthine workings of his new family life. And eventually, they forgave him his failings as a parent. The inevitable bruising that accompanied their own aging has softened them, leaving them less harsh about his shortcomings and more able to appreciate his inattentive amiability.

Ten years ago, on Yom Kippur, in my yearly attempt

to atone for pain I might have caused people in my life, I sent him a letter apologizing for the ways I had injured him, taking our children away and behaving selfishly toward someone who had always done his best to love me. I slid over the complexities; it was now more than four decades after our separation and no longer necessary to say that he drank too much or that I had taken a lover. Or that I felt trapped in the suburbs, while he was proud to show his father how successful he was in his big house. Or that neither of us knew how to speak truthfully and clearly to one another. I left all that out. I just wanted him to know what was, finally, important. I was sorry and ashamed and owed him my apology.

His response was awkward, but, like him, trustworthy. "Well, it all turned out. I got to spend my life with R., and you got to do whatever the hell it was that you wanted. So don't worry about it. But thank you for writing the letter. It was good to get it."

When his wife died and he was no longer able to live alone, our daughters moved him to a residential facility near them where he could be assisted in his living. Receiving help has been difficult for him, a child of the depression, a soldier in World War II, a believer in getting up, dusting off, and moving forward in life. This once-sophisticated New Yorker, now frail, was now playing bingo and poker and going to a twice-a-week happy hour.

He and I reentered one another's lives then. Apart

from the weddings or illnesses of our daughters, we hadn't been in direct contact for nearly fifty years. But now, when I go to visit, the four of us have dinner together.

He moves into the restaurant slowly, leaning heavily on his walker. Settling into his seat, he first orders his essential vodka martini—very dry with a twist—then leans back, looks appraisingly at me, and says with a familiar heartiness, "Still looking good, old woman. I'm glad to see you." Nothing fancy. He was never one for fancy words, but I know his clumsy efforts are genuine. And it is good to see him. I am glad too.

I'm always careful to sit beside him because his hearing is poor and mine only a little better. We talk about our own personal "back in the day." When we saw Laurence Olivier in *The Entertainer.* When we sang show tunes at a piano bar till closing. When I had my emergency appendectomy. Both of us careful not to say anything that referred to our terrible final days, just the early times when we still were happy together.

I watch as the conversation with our daughters volleys back and forth, often too fast for him to follow, and when a question is lobbed in his direction, he can't always respond quickly enough. But in his efforts to be a part of the conversation, he begins a story that he thinks is relevant to what is being said.

Our daughters have concluded that he's repeating

himself. "Tell us what you see, Mom," they say, correctly assuming that I, as an old person, will have the insight that they need.

What I saw was they were too fast, and he was too slow. I identify with him, patient with his repetitions since I too have been gently reminded by friends that I've told that one before. And perhaps preparing for the time when I too may be limited to the same six or seven stories because I know how they go, and the others are just a bit out of reach.

One of his memories is witnessing my mother being critical of me—perhaps it was my housekeeping or my mothering or my cooking, I no longer remember. He firmly let my mother know that since he was sixteen years older than I was, he was closer to her age than to mine and therefore free to insist that she be respectful of me and of our marriage. He is the hero and a good husband in the telling. He recounts it proudly, his understanding of how he defended me to a woman I was then still struggling to please and separate from. I love listening to his stories now. Both to what he says and to what he means.

Another oft-told story took place during the years he was in the good marriage, in a moment when his wife had called his mother to wish her a happy eighty-fifth birthday and he impulsively went to get his violin to play "My Yiddishe Mama" to her over the telephone. He tells it the same way each time, unable to access the words that might express his appreciation for the violin lessons she encouraged him to take all those years before and how he used the bow and strings instead of words to tell her that he loved her.

And there are my stories as well. When our youngest became ill, I called to tell him, and without hesitation or questions, he simply said, "What do you need? What can I do?"

He was never a man given to asking why things happened as they did, but moved directly to what needed to happen next.

When she was convalescing, he asked me what he could do to let her know he was, in his words, "in her corner."

"Go to a card shop, buy a few dozen funny cards, and send one to her every day. She'll enjoy getting the mail and hearing from you," I advised.

He did. The cards were his words, the ones he was never comfortable saying. He is a soft man, a garrulous man, a courteous, friendly man. He managed to find his way past a powerful father, and I, past a controlling mother. We both found our way into lives that fit us and allowed us our weaknesses.

Now, when my younger daughter visits him, she brings CDs of Frank Sinatra and Édith Piaf so that they can sing his favorite songs together. Her sister takes him for long drives in the mountains because he can manage the walker and oxygen in her car. They both bring their best selves as they accompany this old man as he moves toward his death.

I joined the three of them at what will probably be his last Thanksgiving dinner. We spent some time alone before our daughters joined us, and I took the opportunity to tell him again how deeply sorry I was to have broken his heart all those decades ago. He nodded with appreciation for my words and the gallantry that so defines him. His absence of emotional language was such a source of frustration for me once, but I have lived long enough to hear his words in the silences.

Nearly a half century ago, I broke our original nuclear family apart in an urgent reach for my own freedom. His dying has brought the four of us back into loving symmetry. The original gangsters.

FOREVER AFTER

Several months ago, there was a minor earthquake, a not-uncommon phenomenon given that I live in the San Francisco Bay Area. The brief but terrifying experience of feeling the ground trembling beneath my feet left me with strengthened resolve to finally get my earthquake kit together. I had lived through the Loma Prieta earthquake of 1989, standing in the doorway as instructed, arms pressed against the doorjamb looking like a terrified Samson holding up the temple. Now my procrastination had to end.

I printed out all the government-approved lists of the necessary items, compared them, made a master list, and began my preparations, comforted by the concreteness of this process, precautions I can take that may, just may, affect the outcome of a catastrophic earthquake. Flashlights. Whistles. First aid kit. Sturdy shoes. I can do this.

I gathered pliers, duct tape, toothbrushes, and toothpaste (like an S-and-M dungeon, but with good oral hygiene) for my emergency grab-and-go bag.

But I can't prepare for the specific big one. My personal earthquake. I don't know if it will come with a bang (hopefully in my sleep), in a trickle (with declining physical or mental capacities), or with a serious disease, requiring me, in the military language of illness, to decide whether to do "battle" with whatever it is.

Nevertheless, even with counting my steps, flossing my teeth, and eating more kale than I ever wanted, there is the bigger decision that all this masks. I want to be able to determine the circumstances under which I continue my life. But the decision to be or not to be is not simply my own. Or at least not legally anyway. When I was young, any woman wanting to access a legal abortion needed both her husband and her doctor to approve the procedure. Life is sacred, our opponents bellowed. *Our Bodies, Ourselves!* we roared back. Their rules grew up around our lives. And abortion was possible only in the first trimester, for women who could afford to pay for the procedure.

Now, a dishearteningly similar conversation about who makes decisions about women's bodies is echoed in debates about end-of-life choices. We need to confirm that we are near the end of our lives, or too impaired to function without help that we often can't afford to get, or not simply depressed, the combination of sorrow and old age considered an insufficient reason to end one's life. There is an underground, of course, just as there was in the 1960s, when women who wanted abortions were provided with the ability to access them. There will always be an underground. But that's simply a first step of resistance, not an end point, which would be a respectful policy.

The father of my two daughters, an intrepid old man, has lived too long. He is ninety-eight now and has confessed to me that he awakens in the morning with another day stretching out before him, one in which he can no longer walk, breathe without oxygen, remember much, or drink anything but Ensure (and an occasional vodka martini), needing to give himself a good pep talk so he can move into the day with the best spirits possible. He's lovely that way. But I'm not. I don't want to live too long. I want to be in charge of when enough is simply enough.

My death will be hard on my daughters no matter how it comes. Not on me. They would manage the loss of me more easily if I had a slow, tender decline before I popped off. That way they could have all the anticipatory conversations, review all the tender memories, offer the small, kind acts of love—everything they are both doing now that allows them to release their dying father. It's working for them, but I'm not at all sure it's working for him.

Then there is the me who is now dead. That will require a decision about what is formally defined as "the disposition of the body." I have to decide about my body's disposition or leave that complex task for my daughters. When they asked their dad how he wanted his remains to be remaindered, his response was a brusque "Dead is dead. Do whatever you want."

While I certainly agree with him that dead is dead, I need to give this a bit more thought. I have spent decades thinking about how I want to inhabit my political and spiritual Jewish self, but as nontraditional as many of my choices have been, I suspect there may be a comfort in being disposed of the way Jews have traditionally handled this process over the centuries.

I'm a congregant in a small synagogue that has just the right blend of erudition, spontaneity, music, and politics to make Jewish sense to me, and there is, in this as in most congregations, a small group of volunteers called the *chevra kadisha,* who ensure that the departed (that would be me) is ritually cleansed, shrouded, and prepared for traditional Jewish burial.

The process is embedded in the belief that the human body is sacred and holy, and that even when the body is deceased, it's still compared to an impaired Torah scroll that while no longer useable, still retains its holiness.

I don't think about my body as a holy vessel. Well, I did once when I practiced yoga and meditation and did colonic cleanses. That was a mercifully brief period, very long ago, and there is no need to go into it now. But I like the image of myself as an impaired scroll, my body akin to a Torah, even when I won't be in it anymore because I'll be dead. And naked. I'll be washed, all my crevices thoroughly cleansed, rinsed three times, and dressed in traditional burial clothing. Often there is music or chanting going on while moving through each stage. That seems lovely.

My eldest daughter has asked to be a part of the ritual, called taharah, or at least be allowed to witness it. My younger is a bit more like her dad; ritual doesn't provide a significant source of comfort, and she'll probably demur. But once I'm ceremonially cleansed and wrapped in white linen, the next hurdle presents itself. Am I going into the ground or into the furnace?

When he dies, my daughters have decided to cremate their father as a way of respecting his lifelong nihilism. My parents and younger brother are in lot N, row 4 in a large cemetery across the country, but in the intervening decades since their deaths, I've never flown east to stand before their markers. Not even once. That is not to say that each of them and our unique relationships don't remain alive within me. My mother especially. Super close. I hear her, more than eighteen years after her death, more than I even want to. But there is still something comforting about her voice, even though it's still telling me the same things she told me fifty years ago. Stand up straight. Don't fill up on bread and water before the main course arrives. Make me proud. Make yourself proud. Varied bossy stuff like that. The same kind of stuff I still say to my daughters.

A lot of institutionally affiliated Jews have a very hard time—understandably so—with the choice of cremation. I feel a bit uneasy about being burned up, especially given that the Holocaust was a central historic reality of my lifetime. But I do like the idea of ashes, of something tangible left of me. My eldest daughter might want an ornate urn with some me in it. My youngest will probably opt for a teary scattering someplace, preferring framed pictures to an accumulation of leftover me. But there is no place that contains my history, holds memory, and represents a sense of continuity. Thirty-three years ago, when my beloved died, she was cremated and scattered in our backyard, where mourners came with small plants to mix with her ashes in the fertile soil. That felt perfect. Generative. Respectful. We marked both the ending of her and the beginning of new life. But it's decades later and I'm not there anymore. I live in a condominium and am surrounded by an emotionally neutral landscape. There are places that matter to my daughters though, and I suppose they will agree on where to scatter the part of me that is not resting comfortably in a decorative urn.

Sometimes in synagogue during the recitation of the kaddish, a time when mourners say the name of a beloved who has died, I whisper my name—just to hear how it sounds folded into the names of the dead filling the sanctuary. Because there will be such a day. I am preparing to become an ancestor. And it will be sooner rather than later. I'm certain my daughters will continue to hear my voice for as long as they can hear. And that's what I want. To be heard. Maybe deciding to place my remains in a specific spot they can visit will provide them some comfort. Or having an urn and some scattering. Either way is OK, just so long as my voice continues to ring in their ears. Permanently.

ACKNOWLEDGMENTS

I'd like to start with thanks to my writing group. Frances Reid, Nan Gefen, and Nancy Stoller read this book more times than was reasonable to ask and were rigorous in their feedback and generous in their support. Every word has passed muster from a diligent and appreciative crew.

In 1989, eight women gathered to form a woman's circle. We named ourselves the Wandering Menstruals and have met on the first Saturday of every month since then. We were Nan Gefen, Jane Arie., Marinell Eva, Marcia Freedman z"l, Arlene Shmaeff z"l, Linda Wilson, Sandy Boucher, and me. Now, there are four of us who continue this life-centering tradition. I am grateful to each of you.

Then there are my old lady girlfriends. Donna Korones, Naomi Newman, Jan Holmgren, Rochelle Towers, Eva Pettersson, Elana Dykewomon, Barbara Zoloth, Sharon Washington, Lorraine Bonner, Penny Rosenwasser, and Lauren Chaitkin. And the men. In 2007, I was given the unexpected gift of a beloved godson, Evan Blumensweig, by his mothers, Sue Swigart and Nicole Bloom. They expanded my family and my heart. Jonathan Omer-Man, David Pittman, and my son-in-law, Tim McAlee, have been present at all the significant markers of these past decades. Each of you has deepened my life, sharpened my thinking, and opened my heart. Thank you for the walks, the conversations, the Caesar salads, the encouragement, and the love.

An enthusiastic shout-out to the women of Girl Friday Productions who helped this book into being, whose commitment to women's voices served as the perfect vehicle for my stories. Their critical intelligence, meticulous attention to every detail, and patience in the process helped to guide *The Kitchen Is Closed* into your hands. I'm grateful to each of the women who lent their skills to this process. Anna Katz "got" my voice and edited me to a tee. Kristin Duran navigated the details of the book's development step by painstaking step. Katie Meyers guided the marketing, and Abi Pollokoff produced what you are holding in your hands. Thank you all.

ABOUT THE AUTHOR

Photo © Alison Butler

Sandra Butler grew up in a 1940s suburb and was raised to be a conventional woman, mother, and wife. After Butler was married at eighteen and divorced at twenty-six, she and her two young daughters were catapulted into the changing world of the 1960s. Immersed in the antiwar and civil rights movements, she found her political and psychological foundation with the women's liberation movement of the 1970s. She began college in her midthirties, which led to graduate study, three books, two films, and decades of meetings, organizing, and community building.

Butler is the author of *Conspiracy of Silence: The Trauma of Incest*. Her second book, *Cancer in Two Voices*, coauthored with Barbara Rosenblum, was the winner of the 1991 Lambda Literary Award. She is also the coproducer of the award-winning documentaries *Cancer in Two Voices* (1994) and *Ruthie and Connie: Every Room in the House* (2002). Both films screened in Toronto, Montreal, Berlin, and Sundance and are widely used for training and educational purposes. In her late seventies with two adult daughters, Butler completed her third book, *It Never Ends: Mothering Middle-Aged Daughters*, with Nan Fink Gefen.

There is a through line that has informed her vision as both a writer and an activist. Each book has centered on the need to move issues relevant to women and girls still in the shadows into the public sphere. *Conspiracy of Silence* brought attention to issues of incest and sexual violation; *Cancer in Two Voices* frankly explored how a lesbian couple navigates the death of a partner; and *It Never Ends* illuminated the first-person experience of aging mothers and their daughters and the challenges and adaptations that have emerged over the lifespan of the relationship.

Butler now lives in Phoenix, Arizona, after spending nearly fifty years in the San Francisco Bay Area.

Made in the USA
Las Vegas, NV
24 July 2022

52078986R10106